Resolving An Inconsistency In Economic Theory

John P. Barrados, Ph.D. (Columbia)

Studies In Economic Theory

Order this book online at www.trafford.com
or email orders@trafford.com

Most Trafford titles are also available at major online book retailers.

Print information available on the last page.

ISBN: 978-1-4269-2961-8 (sc)
ISBN: 978-1-4907-3760-7 (e)

Library of Congress Control Number: 2010903165

Trafford rev. 07/06/2015

Trafford
PUBLISHING®   www.trafford.com

North America & international
toll-free: 1 888 232 4444 (USA & Canada)
fax: 812 355 4082

Contents

There Is An Inconsistency In Orthodox Price Systems

We uncover in this book an inconsistency in economic theory. This is an inconsistency that characterizes orthodox theoretical price systems and which suppresses the general economic logic of the systems.

We shall focus in much of the book on this inconsistency as it characterizes the orthodox classical system which is a long-run system. However, we shall set out a revised classical system through which we shall resolve the inconsistency in the orthodox classical system.

Yet while much of our focus will be on the classical system, this is with the broader aim of isolating the general economic logic that should underlie all price systems including macroeconomic systems such as the Keynesian system.

Consequently, this book deals with the general logic that should underlie all price systems rather than with the specific forms of behavior of individual systems.

As discussed, we shall develop a revised classical system; and a substantial part of our analysis will be concerned with contrasting this revised classical system with the orthodox classical system and the Keynesian is system.

However, in contrasting these systems we shall be contrasting only the general logic of the systems rather than contrasting the specific forms of behavior of the systems. Let us describe the inconsistency that we uncover in orthodox price systems, systems we represent by the orthodox classical system.

Price systems are necessarily *subject* to limitation in resources. Hence the behavior in the systems should be behavior that ensures that the systems are *consistent* with limitation in resources.

We define this as behavior that ensures that the quantities of commodities demanded and supplied in price systems, in being limited by the systems' given resources, each sum to the systems' limited or given resources in order to exhaust these resources.

Consequently, we take consistency with limited resources of price systems to be reflected in the quantities of commodities demanded and supplied each summing to the systems' limited resources to exhaust these resources.

Next, since consistency with limitation in resources applies across all price systems, we may look on consistency with limited resources as reflecting the general logic of the systems.

We shall take the orthodox classical system, which we shall refer to as Model A, as representative of orthodox microeconomic price systems. As well, we shall set out a revised classical system, to be referred to as Model B, which we shall take as representative of our new microeconomic systems.

Let us now consider the orthodox classical system Model A which we shall set out in detail in Chapter 3. We shall find that the behavior in this system does not ensure that the system is consistent with limitation in resources.

This is because an aspect to the behavior of individuals and firms, which we shall describe in Chapter 1.4, is missing from Model A. This is the aspect to behavior that should ensure that the system is consistent with limitation in resources. Next, all price systems must reflect consistency with limitation in resources.

Hence since the aspect to behavior referred to is missing from Model A, this results in the system being made consistent with limitation in resources in a non-behavioral manner rather than by the behavior in the system. This brings inconsistency into Model A.

This is because consistency of a system with limitation in resources, or consistency of the system's general logic, should be ensured by the behavior in the system and hence by the system's demand and supply functions.

Model A, however, is made consistent with limitation in resources in a non-behavioral manner rather than by the behavior in the system. Model A does indeed reflect the *general logic* of price systems in reflecting consistency with limitation in resources.

However, Model A does not reflect the general *economic* logic of price systems; since consistency of the system with limitation in resources is not ensured by the behavior in the system.

Instead, consistency with limitation in resources is ensured in a non-behavioral manner. This accounts for the inconsistency we have uncovered in the system.

Let us now consider our revised form of Model A which we refer to as Model B. We shall find that consistency with limitation in resources is ensured in Model B by the system's behavior or economic rationale. This will mean that Model B, unlike Model A, will reflect the general *economic* logic of price systems.

Hence through Model B, our revised classical system, we shall resolve the inconsistency of Model A. This is because we shall bring the aspect to behavior that is missing from Model A into Model B. We may summarize the analysis of this book in the following way.

We shall establish that the general logic of Model A, as reflected in consistency of the system with limitation in resources, stems is ensured in a non-behavioral manner rather than by the behavior in the system.

This brings inconsistency into Model A since this system does not reflect the general *economic* logic that should underlie all price systems.

Whereas we shall establish that the general logic of Model B as also reflected in consistency of the system with limitation in resources, stems from the system's behavior or economic rationale. This means that Model B, unlike Model A, reflects the general *economic* logic that should characterize all price systems.

This accounts for us resolving through Model B, the inconsistency of Model A; and through Model B, we shall come upon a more general approach to price systems compared to the orthodox approach that characterizes Model A.

This is due to Model B reflecting the new aspect to behavior described in Chapter 1.4 and hence the general economic logic that should characterize all price systems.

On the other hand, this new aspect to behavior and hence this general economic logic is missing from Model A. This restricts the generality of the latter system compared to Model B.

This difference between the systems accounts for Model B being characterized by a more general approach to microeconomics compared to the orthodox approach to microeconomics of Model A. Let us illustrate this by contrasting the two systems.

In resolving the inconsistency of Model A through Model B, we shall rid the latter system of the Say's Law that characterizes Model A. This is a form of the Law that restricts Model A to long-run states.

Hence it is through Model B's more general microeconomics that we rid this system of Model A's Say's Law. Consequently, Model B has a more general character than Model A since Model B is not restricted like Model A to long-run states by Say's Law. Let us now bring out some implications of this analysis for the Keynesian system.

Model B and the Keynesian system are both rid of Model A's Say's Law that restricts the latter system to long-run states. However, as discussed, we accomplish this through ridding Model B of the inconsistency we uncover in Model A.

This is by our approaching Model B through microeconomic analysis which accounts for this system being wholly microeconomic in character.

Keynes also rid his system of Model A's form of Say's Law that restricts the latter system to long-run states but this is accomplished through macroeconomic analysis. This is through Keynes allowing the aggregate demand and supply of commodities in his system to diverge.

However, this accounts for the microeconomics of the real part of the Keynesian system being suppressed, this being the part of the system that deals with aggregate demand and supply variables. References to the Keynesian system throughout the book are solely to this part of the system.

Hence we arrive at a similar conclusion through Model B and the Keynesian system. This is that both of these systems are rid of Model A's form of Say's Law that restricts the latter system to long-run states. However, we shall accomplish this through microeconomic analysis whereas Keynes accomplished this through macroeconomic analysis.

This means that Keynes' macroeconomics is, as it were, a short-cut to ridding his system of Model A's form of Say's Law. This, however, is a short-cut that is forced on the Keynesian system. Let us discuss why this is the case.

Through Model B we resolve the inconsistency of Model A; and in so doing, we come upon a more general approach to microeconomics compared to the orthodox approach of Model A. This more general approach to microeconomics allows us to rid Model B of Model A's Say's Law that restricts the latter system to long-run states.

Consequently, through Model B we avoid Keynes' macroeconomic short-cut to ridding his system of Model A's Say's Law. This short-cut accounts for the microeconomics of the real part of the Keynesian system being suppressed.

On the other hand, we rid Model B of Model A's Say's Law through microeconomic analysis. This accounts for Model B being wholly microeconomic in character. Hence we rid Model B of Model A's Say's Law while preserving Model B as a wholly microeconomic system.

Whereas Keynes rid his system of Model A's Say's Law in a manner that accounts for the microeconomics of the real part of his system being suppressed. We can now bring out the overall consequences of the inconsistency of Model A for this system and the Keynesian system.

This inconsistency mars Model A by accounting for this system being restricted to long-run states by Say's Law. This inconsistency, however, is resolved through Model B. Hence this latter system is not restricted by the Law to long-run states. Let us next consider the Keynesian system.

Keynes as we shall discuss in Chapter 8 bypassed, rather than resolve, the inconsistency of Model A. This we shall find accounts for the Keynesian system being rid of Model A's Say's Law that restricts the latter system to long-run states.

Keynes' approach, however, results in the microeconomics of the real part of the Keynesian system being suppressed. On the other hand through Model B we resolve, rather than bypass, the inconsistency of Model A. This accounts for Model B being wholly microeconomic in character.

We have now brought out the essential contribution of this book. This is that in resolving through Model B the inconsistency we uncover in Model A, we arrive through Model B at a more general approach to microeconomics compared to the microeconomics of Model A.

This is due to the new aspect behavior that we bring into Model B, an aspect to behavior that is missing from orthodox systems.

This accounts for us resolving through Model B the problem of Model A being restricted to long-run states by Say's Law. Moreover, this is accomplished while ensuring that Model B is wholly microeconomic in character.

Keynes also resolved the problem of Model A being restricted to long-run states by Say's Law. Keynes, however, did not accomplish this by resolving the inconsistency of Model A as is done in this book. Instead, Keynes through his macroeconomic approach bypassed this inconsistency in his system.

This approach allowed Keynes to rid his system of the problem of Model A being restricted to long-run states by Say's Law. However, this is accomplished in a manner that accounts for the microeconomics of the real part of the Keynesian system being suppressed. There is a further key part of our analysis to be brought out.

We shall find that our resolving the inconsistency of Model A through Model B allows us to deal in a more general manner with the budget constraints of price systems compared to how these constraints are dealt with in orthodox analysis. This accounts for Model B being characterized by a more general type of budget constraint compared to the budget constraint of Model A.

This results in Model B being rid of Model A's Say's Law that is not a true identity and which restricts the latter system to long-run states. This is then replaced in Model B with a correct form of the Law that is a true identity and which cannot possibly restrict this system to long-run states.

In sum, through resolving the inconsistency of Model A through Model B we also resolve the issue of Say's Law. That is, the issue of the Law restricting the orthodox classical system Model A to long-run states. This finding as will now be discussed will assist us in explaining in Chapter 6.14 why Say's Law became a problematic issue in the literature.

Economists generally focus directly on the Law in dealing with the issue of the restriction of Model A by the Law to long-run states. This approach, however, cannot satisfactorily resolve this issue.

This is because to satisfactorily resolve this issue, we need to resolve the inconsistency we uncover in Model A; since this inconsistency is what brings a form of the Law into Model A that restricts this system to long-run states.

This is the approach we follow in this book through Model B which accounts for us satisfactorily resolving in this book the issue of Say's Law restricting the orthodox classical system to long-run states.

Finally, most of the findings of the book stem from the new aspect to behavior that we shall set out in Chapter 1.4. This new aspect to behavior is of such generality that it not only allows us to resolve the inconsistency we uncovered in the orthodox classical system.

This new aspect to behavior applies across all price systems and, in principle it can bring a unity to price systems irrespective of the differing forms of behavior of individual systems.

My introduction to economic analysis was at McGill University where I benefitted considerably from courses in economic theory given by Professors Earl F. Beach and David McCord Wright.

I am also indebted to Professors William S. Vickrey and Phillip David Cagan of Columbia University. I gained much from their economic theory courses and from their help with a

Preface

dissertation on price theory that I wrote at Columbia. An outcome of my work in price theory has been a number of published papers as well as the present book.

John P. Barrados,
Ottawa, Ontario,
Canada.
March, 2014.

Chapter 1

Uncovering The General Economic Logic Of Price Systems

1.1 Introduction

We shall discuss in an overall way in this chapter, the inconsistency we uncover in Model A, the orthodox classical price system. As well, we shall discuss how we shall resolve this inconsistency through Model B, our revised classical system.

Model A, the orthodox classical system, was developed in neoclassical analysis but is also widely taken as a formal version of the classical price system.

Hence while we may refer to Model A as both classical and neoclassical we shall find it convenient to take it as a classical system. Nonetheless, there are digressions in parts of the book on Model A when this system is taken specifically as a neoclassical system.[1]

We shall also, as discussed, develop a revised form of Model A which we refer to as Model B. That is, the latter system is our revised classical system. We shall approach both of these systems as market systems hence basing the systems on market demand and supply functions.

That is, we do not develop our systems in detail from the maximizing behavior of the individual and the firm although this may readily be done.

We may, however, look on this book as dealing through Model B with how a consistent transition is to be made from the maximizing behavior of the individual and the firm to the theory of market price determination as will be discussed in the conclusion of the book.

---

[1] This system appears in many places in the literature being called at times a classical system and at other times a neoclassical system. See, for example, W.B.Hickman, "The Determinacy of Absolute Prices in Classical Economic Theory," *Econometrica*, 1950, where it is called a classical system. However, see Don Patinkin, *Money, Interest, And Prices* (2nd. ed., Harper and Row, New York, 1965), esp. Ch. VIII, where it is called a neoclassical system.

Model B, our revised classical system puts Model A, the orthodox classical system into a more general form. This is accomplished by our bringing into Model B, an aspect to the behavior of individuals and firms that is missing from Model A.

This new aspect to behavior is of such a general character that it allows us to preserve in Model B the basic character of Model A. This is in the sense that Model A and Model B are both long-run microeconomic systems.

Yet Model B will have a more general character than Model A. This is because Model B will reflect the aspect to behavior that is missing from Model A.

This is the aspect to behavior that ensures that a price system reflects behavior that is consistent with limitation in resources. This will account for Model B reflecting the general economic logic that should underlie all price systems.

On the other hand, this aspect to behavior is missing from Model A which causes the general economic logic of price systems to be suppressed in the system. This brings inconsistency into Model A. This chapter also covers in a preliminary way a basic consequence of our resolving the inconsistency of Model A through Model B.

This is reflected in Model B being rid of an incorrect form of Say's Law that characterizes Model A and which restricts this latter system to long-run states. Yet Model B will reflect Say's Law but a correct form of the Law that cannot possibly restrict this system to long-run states.

There will be a great deal of focus in the book on how consistency of price systems is ensured. Hence we shall draw on the well-known "counting rule" that is used to ensure consistency of orthodox price systems. This rule is that the number of independent equations and unknown variables in a system must be equal.

We shall find that while all price systems must meet this rule, this must be ensured by the behavior in the systems. This we shall find is the case with Model B on account of the new aspect to behavior that we shall bring into this system.

However, since this aspect to behavior is missing from Model A, this system meets this rule in a non-behavioral manner through Say's Law.

Consequently, while both Model A and Model B both meet the counting rule, Model A meets this rule on account of the non-behavioral Say's Law. On the other hand, Model B meets this rule due to the behavior in the system.

2

This results in Model B having a more general character that Model A which will be reflected in various ways. For example, in Model A being restricted to long-run states by Say's Law whereas Model B is not restricted in this way.

Chapters 1 and 2 will cover in a general way our new approach to price systems and how through this new approach we shall arrive at our revised classical system, Model B.

Then in Chapters 3 and 4, we shall set out the orthodox classical system, Model A, and discuss various problems with the system that have been brought out in the literature. In Chapter 5, we shall set out in detail the rationale of our new approach to price systems.

These analyses of Chapters 1 to 5 will provide the basis to formally set out Model B, our revised classical system, in Chapter 6. Chapter 7 will then be concerned with illustrating some basic properties of Model B.

Chapter 8 will bring out how Keynes in the real part of his system bypassed the inconsistency in Model A. This accounts for the microeconomics of the real part of the Keynesian system being suppressed.

This, to review, is the part of the system that deals with aggregate demand and supply variables; and references to the Keynesian system throughout this book are solely to this real part of the system.

Chapter 9 then takes the analysis of Chapter 8 a step further to establish in more detail why the microeconomics of the real part of the Keynesian system is suppressed.

We shall next discuss in Chapter 10 how we rid Model B of the price level indeterminacy and invalid real-monetary dichotomy of Model A, problems raised by Patinkin. In Chapter 11 we discuss issues concerning consistency of the classical system and finally, we shall provide an overall review of the book in Chapter 12.

1.2 The New And Orthodox Approaches To Price Systems

Let us discuss the orthodox approach to price systems. By the orthodox approach to price systems we mean the approach that is the basis of orthodox microeconomic systems, systems we represent by Model A, the orthodox classical system.

This approach is based on individuals and firms demanding and supplying goods, subject to a budget constraint, to maximize their utility and profit. This behavior, in turn, leads to demand and supply functions that apply to each individual and firm.

These demand and supply functions of individuals and firms are then aggregated to form market demand and supply functions on which market price systems are based. This, of course, is the standard approach to orthodox microeconomic price systems, systems we represent by Model A.

Let us sketch how this approach will be revised in this book though our new systems, systems we represent by Model B, our revised classical system. We shall show that the inconsistency in orthodox price systems uncovered in this book suppresses a key aspect to the behavior of individuals and firms in the systems.

This results in the orthodox or neoclassical-type demand and supply functions, while reflecting the behavior of particular systems, suppressing the general economic logic that should underlie all price systems. This is because the orthodox-type functions do not reflect behavior that is consistent with limitation in resources.

However, through resolving the inconsistency in orthodox price systems that we uncover in this book, we shall bring the aspect to behavior that is missing from these orthodox systems into our new systems. These new systems, to review, are systems that we represent by Model B, our revised classical system.

This will be accomplished through a new type of demand and supply functions. These new functions will not only reflect the behavior of particular systems that stems from the maximizing behavior of individuals and firms.

As well, the functions will capture the general economic logic that should underlie all price systems. This is because our new functions will reflect behavior that is consistent with limitation in resources.

These new functions will account for Model B, our revised classical system, reflecting the general economic logic that should underlie all price systems. On the other hand, Model A, the orthodox classical system does not reflect this general economic logic.

This restricts the generality of Model A compared to Model B which is reflected, for example, in Model A being restricted to long-run states by Say's Law. On the other hand, Model B is not restricted in this way.

4

1.3 The Inconsistency In The Orthodox Classical Price System

We shall base Model A on market demand and supply functions that stem from the underlying maximizing behavior of the individual and the firm. However, the system is found to be initially inconsistent in that the number of independent equations and the number of unknowns are not initially equal.

Economists then ensure that Model A is consistent. This is usually done by imposing Say's Law on the system to eliminate a surplus equation to equate the number of independent equations and the number of unknowns in the system. However, this is an incorrect use of the Law as is readily established.

Say's Law is a true identity hence no substantive role should be attributed to it in a system in order to preserve the Law as a true identity. However, the Law in Model A is given the substantive role of ensuring consistency of the system.

Hence the Law in Model A is not a true identity which explains why it is not a correct form of the Law; and it is this incorrect Say's Law that restricts Model A to long-run states. True, economists in setting out Model A write Say's Law as an identity.

However, this identity is misused in Model A in being given the substantive role described. This explains why we conclude that there is an incorrect or misused form of the Law in Model A; since a correct form of the Law should not be given the substantive role described.

We must emphasize that Say's Law in being an identity or truism cannot of itself be incorrect or inconsistent. However, we shall find it convenient to refer to Model A as being characterized by an incorrect form of the Law.

This is in the sense that the Law in Model A is misused in the manner described to account for the Law in Model A not being a true identity.

Now imposing this incorrect Say's Law on Model A allows us to solve for the system's equilibrium quantities of commodities and equilibrium prices. However, we must assume that Model A is *subject* to limitation in resources.

Hence the quantities that we solve for must sum to the system's limited resources to exhaust these resources. This means that in making Model A consistent in meeting the counting rule, we also ensure *consistency* of the system with limitation in resources.

5

This is because consistency with limitation in resources is also reflected in the quantities that are determined in Model A summing to the system's limited resources to exhaust these resources. As a result, in making Model A consistent in meeting the counting rule, we ensure that the system is consistent with limitation in resources.

However, to be satisfactorily ensured, consistency with limitation in resources in price systems should be ensured by the behavior of individuals and firms and hence by the systems' demand and supply functions. We can now bring out in detail the inconsistency that we have uncovered in Model A, the orthodox classical price system.

Consistency with limitation in resources, to review, is reflected in the individual quantities of commodities determined in a system summing to the system's limited resources. Next, consistency with limited resources should be ensured by the behavior or economic rationale of the system.

Instead, consistency with limitation in resources is ensured in Model A as a result of the non-behavioral Say's Law being imposed on the system to eliminate a surplus equation. This is the inconsistency that we have uncovered in Model A, an inconsistency that is economic in character.

This is because it arises because an aspect to the behavior of individuals and firms is missing from the system. This is the aspect to behavior that should ensure that the system is consistent with limitation in resources.

We shall, however, resolve Model A's inconsistency through Model B; since consistency of the latter system with limitation in resources will be ensured by the system's behavior or economic rationale. This is because it will be ensured by Model B's demand and supply functions.

Moreover, Model B's demand and supply functions will automatically ensure that the system meets the counting rule. This means that consistency of Model B is ensured in quite a different way from how it is ensured in Model A.

Consistency of Model A is ensured by Say's Law being imposed on the system to eliminate a surplus equation. This accounts for the system meeting the counting rule in that the number of independent equations and unknowns are equal.

This, however, gives the non-behavioral Say's Law precedence over economic consistency in ensuring consistency of the system with limited resources. This, however, will be resolved through Model B; since consistency of the latter system will stem from the system's general economic consistency. This is because

Model B's behavior or economic rationale, through the system's demand and supply functions, will ensure that the system meets the counting rule.

This will result in Model B, our revised classical system, having a more general character than Model A, the orthodox classical system; and through Model B, we shall resolve the inconsistency we uncovered in Model A.

As well, we shall simultaneously resolve through Model B, the longstanding issue of Say's Law restricting the orthodox classical system to long-run states.

1.4 The Aspect To Behavior That Is Missing From The Orthodox Classical System

We have discussed how inconsistency arises in Model A because consistency of the system with limited resources is ensured in a non-behavioral manner. This is a reflection of an economic inconsistency in the system.

This is because it reflects how Model A's demand and supply functions, and hence the behavior in the system does not ensure that the system is consistent with limitation in resources. Instead, consistency of Model A with limitation in resources is ensured as a result of Say's Law being imposed on the system.

This means that an aspect to the behavior of individuals and firms is missing from Model A. This is the aspect to behavior that should ensure that the system is consistent with limitation in resources.

We may best bring out this aspect to behavior by referring to a new type of demand and supply functions to be set out later in the book, functions that will be the basis for Model B, our revised classical system.

These functions will reflect the aspect to behavior that will ensure that our new systems, as represented by Model B, are consistent with limitation in resources. Let us describe this new aspect to behavior.

This new aspect to behavior is reflected in our taking individuals and firms to be aware that their resources are limited. Hence in determining their commodity demands and supplies, they act in light of this awareness. This is through individuals and firms determining quantities of commodities demanded and supplied that exhaust their resources.

This aspect to behavior that we have described is missing from Model A, the orthodox classical system which, as will be discussed more fully in Chapter 11.2, creates a gap in the behavioral content of the system.

However, we shall bring this aspect to behavior into Model B, our revised classical system; and through Model B, we shall resolve the inconsistency that we have uncovered in Model A. This will bring a more general approach to microeconomics into Model B compared to the approach to microeconomics of Model A.

This will ensure that Model B reflects the general economic logic that should characterize all price systems. On the other hand, this general economic logic is suppressed in Model A which brings the inconsistency we have uncovered into the system.

Finally, as we discussed, the new aspect to behavior that we shall bring into our new systems is reflected in our taking individuals and firms to be aware that their resources are limited. Hence in determining their commodity demands and supplies, they act in light of this awareness.

This is through individuals and firms determining quantities of commodities demanded and supplied that exhaust their resources. Next, we shall approach budget constraints in this book by dealing with the limited resources that give rise to these budget constraints.

This means that we may also refer to the new aspect to behavior of our new systems in the following way: this new aspect to behavior is reflected in our taking individuals and firms to be aware that they are subject to a budget constraint.

Hence in determining their commodity demands and supplies, they act in light of this awareness. This is through individuals and firms determining quantities of commodities demanded and supplied that exhaust their budget constraints.

1.5 Remarks On The New Aspect To Behavior Of Model B

We shall as we progress cover in detail the new aspect to behavior that we shall bring into Model B. Let us, however, now discuss a key property of this aspect to behavior. This aspect to behavior has two facets.

First, it reflects how we take individuals and firms to be aware that their resources are limited. Second, they act in light of their awareness that their resources are limited. This is through individuals and firms determining quantities of commodities demanded and supplied that each exhaust their limited resources.

Next, as will be discussed in Chapter 6.8, a precondition for the existence of this second facet to the behavior described in Section 1.4 is the first facet to this behavior. Namely, that individuals and firms be aware that their resources are limited.

Hence we shall bring the overall aspect to behavior described in Section 1.4 into Model B by first ensuring that individuals and firms in this system are aware that their resources limited.

This as will be discussed in Chapter 6.8 will then bring the second facet to the behavior described into Model B. We shall thereby bring the overall behavior described in Section 1.4 into Model B. On the other hand, we shall find that the condition that individuals and firms be aware that their resources are limited is suppressed in Model A.

This causes the second facet to the behavior described to be suppressed in Model A. This results in the overall behavior described in Section 1.4 being suppressed in Model A. This accounts for the inconsistency we have uncovered in the system.

Whereas as will be discussed in Chapter 6.8, the overall behavior described in Section 1.4 will be brought into Model B. This explains why through Model B, we shall resolve the inconsistency of Model A. There is yet, however, a further basic aspect of our analysis to consider.

We shall have to bring out how the suppression in Model A of the new aspect to behavior described influences the system's demand and supply functions. By the same token, we shall also have to bring out how our bringing into Model B this new aspect to behavior influences this system's demand and supply functions.

We shall find that the quantities of commodities demanded and supplied in both Model A and Model B are *relative* quantities demanded and *relative* quantities supplied.

This accounts for both systems reflecting consistency with limitation in resources. This is because these quantities in both systems adjust in a relative manner to always exhaust the systems' limited resources.

However, we shall find that the quantities of commodities demanded and supplied in Model A are transformed into relative quantities demanded (supplied) as a result of the system being made consistent.

This is through Model A's incorrect Say's Law being imposed on the system to eliminate a surplus equation to ensure consistency of the system. In contrast, the quantities of commodities demanded and supplied in Model B are transformed

9

into relative quantities demanded (supplied) by the behavior in the system. This is because of the new aspect to behavior that we shall bring into this system.

Finally, we shall establish in detail in Chapter 6.8 that Model B reflects this new aspect to behavior. On the other hand, this aspect to behavior is suppressed in Model A as we shall also discuss in detail Chapter 6.9.

As well, we shall discuss in Chapters 6.10 and 6.11 how we can bring this new aspect to behavior into Model B only because this system is rid of Model A's incorrect form of Say's Law. This as we shall establish is a form of the Law that is not a true identity and which restricts the system to long-run states.

1.6 Limitation In Resources And The Budget Constraint Of The Classical System

All price systems are necessarily subject to limitation in resources and Model A, the orthodox classical system should be no exception to this. However, there is no explicit variable in the system that reflects the system's limited resources. We shall now isolate a variable in Model A that we shall take to reflect the system's limited resources.

This will then allow us to deal with how consistency with these limited resources is ensured in Model A. That is, with the issue of how the quantities of commodities demanded and supplied are each made to sum to these limited resources.

Say's Law as we shall discuss in Chapter 3 is imposed on Model A to eliminate a surplus equation to ensure consistency of the system. This is through equating the number of independent equations and unknowns in the system.

Say's Law is an identity between the aggregate demand for commodities (ad) and the aggregate supply (as) of commodities. Economists then conclude that excess demands for commodities anywhere in the system are matched by an equal excess supply elsewhere in the system.

Economists, drawing on long-run analysis then conclude that the relative prices will instantaneously adjust to eliminate this disequilibrium in the various markets of the system without changing overall output or income.

This is a long-run, full-employment overall output or income although there will be frictional unemployment, a consequence of job search. Consequently, Say's Law through the market adjustment process described determines Model A's long-run overall output or income which we shall denote by W.

Now when Model A is written, it is found that there is a surplus equation over the number of unknowns hence the system is initially inconsistent. Say's Law, as we discussed, is then imposed on the system to eliminate this surplus equation which ensures that the system is consistent.

However, since W is imposed on Model A from the outside by Say's Law, this results in W remaining outside the system's behavioral content. That is, outside the system's demand and supply functions.

Hence to review, when we impose Say's Law on Model A we impose W, the system's overall output or income on the system although W remains outside the system's behavioral content. Next, as will now be discussed, the Say's Law that we impose on Model A is a budget constraint.

We may look on the Law as arising from our describing W, the system's overall output or income, alternately as the aggregate demand and the aggregate supply of commodities. Then the individual quantities of commodities demanded in Model A sum to this aggregate demand which is identical to W.

As well, the individual quantities of commodities supplied in Model A sum to this aggregate supply which is also identical to W. This reflects how W accounts for Say's Law becoming a budget constraint in Model A.

Next, budget constraints arise as a result of limitation in resources; and Model A's budget constraint as discussed arises from W. Hence the variable W which is Model A's overall output or income also reflects the system's limited resources. This is a limited *flow* of resources. This brings us to a basic part of our analysis.

We have discussed how the variable W is imposed on Model A by Say's Law with W hence remaining outside the system's behavioral content. We shall now establish that this is on account of the inconsistency we uncover in the system.

This is because this inconsistency results in the new aspect to behavior described in Section 1.4 being suppressed in Model A. Were this new aspect to behavior not suppressed in Model A, it would bring W from outside the behavioral content of Model A into the system's behavioral content.

This is because this new aspect to behavior implies that individuals and firms are aware that their resources W are limited. This requires that these resources be brought into Model A's behavioral content.

11

Since this is how individuals and firms in the system are made aware that that their resources are limited. Hence since W is outside Model A's behavioral content, this means that the new aspect to behavior described in Chapter 1.4 is suppressed in the system.

Consequently, the suppression of this new aspect to behavior in Model A accounts for W being put outside the system's behavioral content. This results in W forming the basis for a budget constraint that is imposed on the system from outside the system. That is, Model A is subject to an external budget constraint. Let us now consider Model B.

Model B is also characterized by the variable W which as in Model A reflects Model B's limited flow of resources. However, we shall incorporate into Model B the new aspect to behavior described in Section 1.4.

This new aspect to behavior as we discussed implies that individuals and firms are aware that their resources are limited. This requires that W be brought into the behavioral content of Model B; since this is how individuals and firms are made aware that their resources are limited

Hence the new aspect to behavior that we bring into Model B moves W from outside the behavioral content of Model A into the behavioral content of Model B. Now the variable W, although moving into the behavioral content of Model B also forms, as it does in Model A, the basis for a budget constraint in Model B.

However, this is an internal budget constraint; since the variable W that gives rise to this budget constraint in Model B is now within the system's behavioral content. Hence Model B's budget constraint in being determined within the system cannot possibly restrict the system to long-run states.

On the other hand, as we discussed, Model A's budget constraint is imposed on the system from the outside by Say's Law. This gives rise to an external budget constraint that restricts the system to long-run states.

We have now isolated the variable W which reflects the overall output or income of both Model A and Model B. As well, W reflects the systems' limited flow of resources; and as such it forms the basis for the budget constraints of both systems.

This means that Model A and Model B, like the generality of price systems, are necessarily subject to limitation in sources. However, the limited resources of Model A and Model B take the form of being reflected in a limited *flow* of resources. This is because these systems are wholly in terms of flow variables.

Hence the limited resources of Model A and Model B must be defined in a manner consistent with the systems being in terms of flow variables. This explains why the limited resources of Model A and Model B take the form of being reflected in a limited flow of resources.

Clearly, the limited resources of more detailed systems would be defined in more general ways to also include, for example, stocks of commodities and other assets.

However, our primary focus in the book is on how consistency with limitation in resources is to be ensured irrespective of how we define these resources; and our definition of the limited resources of our systems is sufficient for this purpose.

Now as we implied earlier, we broaden the meaning of the overall output or income of Model A and Model B to also reflect the systems' limited flow of resources. Next, budget constraints stem from limitation in resources.

Hence the limited flow of resources of Model A and Model B will be the basis for the systems' budget constraints. Let us now focus on the latter system then we shall consider Model A.

Model B's overall output or income as will be discussed in Chapter 7 is determined by the system's behavioral market processes. This means that the budget constraint of Model B, in arising from the system's overall output or income, is also determined by the system's behavioral market processes.

Consequently, Model B's budget constraint is determined within the system by the system's behavioral market processes. Hence this internal budget constraint cannot possibly restrict Model B to long-run states.

Whereas Model A's overall output or income as will also be discussed in Chapter 7 is determined in a non-behavioral manner. This is because it is determined by Say's Law through the non-behavioral market process we described earlier rather than by behavioral market processes as in Model B.

This means that Model A's budget constraint in arising from the system's overall output or income, is also determined in a non-behavioral manner rather than by behavioral market processes.

As a result, Model A's budget constraint is not determined within the system by behavioral market processes as in Model B. This accounts for Model A being characterized by an external budget constraint that restricts the system to long-run states.

On the other hand, as we discussed, Model B is characterized by a budget constraint that is determined within the system by the system's behavioral market processes. Hence this budget constraint cannot possibly restrict the system to long-run states.

We are now in a position to sketch how we shall resolve the issue of Say's Law. This is through our dealing with the Law in Model A and Model B as budget constraints. Next, we shall find that Model A is characterized by a budget constraint that brings an incorrect form of Say's Law into the system.

This incorrect form of the Law restricts Model A to long-run states. However, in resolving the inconsistency of Model A through Model B, we shall bring a correct budget constraint into the latter system.

This budget constraint brings a correct form of the Law into Model B that cannot possibly restrict this system to long-run states. This analysis provides the basis for us to establish in fuller detail in Chapter 9.4 how we resolve the issue of Say's Law.

Moreover, the analysis of this section also brings out in a preliminary way how we shall be able to bring microeconomic and macroeconomic elements into Model B. Now the variable W reflects the overall output or income of Model B. Hence W is a macroeconomic variable that is determined by the system's market processes.

However, we shall find that the new aspect to behavior that we bring into Model B accounts for individuals and firms taking W to reflect their limited flow of resources. This brings W into the behavioral content of Model B where it forms the basis for an internal budget constraint in the system.

This is a budget constraint of relevance to microeconomics since we shall find that individual quantities of commodities demanded (supplied) emerge from it to account for Model B being wholly microeconomic in character.

Consequently, the variable W of Model B has a dual meaning that makes it relevant to both macroeconomics and microeconomics. This will account for Model B being characterized by both microeconomic and macroeconomic aspects.

1.7 Further Comments On The Budget Constraints Of Model A And Model B

We isolated in Section 1.6 the variable W that reflects the overall output or income as well as the limited flow of resources of both Model A and Model B. Yet there is a key difference between the systems.

We shall find that individuals and firms in Model B, on account of the new aspect to behavior described in Chapter 1.4 that we shall bring into the system, will look on the variable W as reflecting their limited flow of resources. This will bring W into the behavioral content of Model B. That is, into the system's demand and supply functions.

Furthermore, on account of this new aspect to behavior that we shall bring into Model B, individuals and firms will act in light of their awareness that their resources are limited.

This will result in individuals and firms determining quantities of commodities demanded and supplied that exhaust their limited resources W. This means that W provides the basis for Model B's budget constraint.

This, however, is an internally-determined budget constraint since the variable W that gives rise to this budget constraint is within Model B's behavioral content. That is within the system's demand and supply functions.

Moreover, we shall find that this internally-determined budget constraint cannot possibly restrict Model B to long-run states. On the other hand as we shall now discuss, Model A is characterized by an external budget constraint that restricts the system to long-run states.

Model A like Model B is also characterized by the variable W which also reflects Model A's limited flow of resources as well as the system's overall output or income.

However, since Model A does not reflect the new aspect to behavior of Model B, W is not brought into the behavioral content of Model A but remains outside the system's behavioral content. That is, outside the system's demand and supply functions.

Yet W also forms the basis for a budget constraint in Model A. But this is an external budget constraint which, we shall establish, is an incorrect form of Say's Law that restricts the system to long-run states.

However, in contrast to Model A, Model B will not be restricted to long-run states by an incorrect form of Say's Law. This is because we shall establish in Chapter 2.7, and confirm in Chapter 6.3, that Model B's internal budget constraint reflects a correct form of Say's Law.

This is a form of the Law that is solely a descriptive device hence it can have no substantive influence in Model B. This means that it cannot possibly restrict the system to long-run states.

Model B does describe long-run states; but this, as we shall establish in Chapter 7.3, is because of the behavior in the

15

system rather than on account of an incorrect form of Say's Law as is the case with Model A.

Consequently, we are able to explain in the following way why Model A reflects an incorrect form of Say's Law that restricts the system to long-run states. While on the other hand, B reflects a correct form of the Law that cannot possibly restrict this system to long-run states.

This is because Model A's Say's Law is an external budget constraint that is imposed on the system from outside the system with this external budget constraint restricting the system to long-run-states. This is because Model A's external budget constraint as we shall establish is an incorrect form of Say's Law since it is not a true identity.

On the other hand, Model B's Say's Law is an internally-determined budget constraint that cannot possibly restrict the system to long-run states.

This is because Model B's internal budget constraint as we shall establish is a correct form Say's Law since it is a true identity. Let us put this analysis in the following way. We deal with Say's Law in Model A and Model B by dealing with the Law in these systems as budget constraints.

Then we show that the Law in Model A is an external budget constraint that restricts the system to long-run states. This will allow us to establish that the Law in Model A is an incorrect form of the Law in not being a true identity.

Next, we show that the Law in Model B is an internal budget constraint that cannot possibly restrict the system to long-run states. This will allow us to establish that the Law in Model B is a correct form of the Law in being a true identity.

Hence we arrive at these findings by dealing with Say's Law in Model A and Model B through dealing with the Law in these systems as budget constraints. This allows us to establish two key points:

First, that the Law in Model A is not a true identity to also explain why it restricts the system to long-run states. Second, that the Law in Model B is a true identity to also explain why it cannot possibly this system to long-run states.

Finally, we discussed how the variable W provides the basis for the budget constraints of Model A and Model B. Now W in reflecting the limited flow of resources of individuals and firms also has a role as an independent variable in the systems' demand and supply functions. Hence it influences the systems' commodity demands and supplies.

However, we shall leave this role of W implicit throughout our analyses. This does not affect the generality of the conclusions of the book. Consequently, we shall focus only on how the variable W provides the basis for the budget constraints of Model A and Model B.

1.8 The Budget Constraints Of Model A, Model B And The Keynesian System

We have established that Say's Law in Model A is a budget constraint that is imposed on the system from the outside; and this budget constraint, in being imposed on the system from the outside, restricts the system to long-run states.

Next, we shall find that both Model B and the Keynesian system are rid of Model A's incorrect form of Say's Law and hence of the external budget constraint that restricts the latter system to long-run states. However, all price systems are necessarily subject to a budget constraint.

Hence we need to ensure that Model B and the Keynesian system remain characterized by budget constraints. Let us discuss how this will be accomplished in both systems beginning first with Model B.

We shall find that the new aspect to behavior that we bring into Model B transforms Model A's external budget constraint into an internal budget constraint in Model B. This is a budget constraint which in being determined within the system cannot possibly restrict Model B to long-run states.

Moreover, this budget constraint ensures that Model B like Model A is wholly microeconomic in character. Let us now consider the Keynesian system. This system is not commonly considered to be subject to an explicit budget constraint.

However, we shall find in Chapter 9.11 that Model A's external budget constraint is also transformed into an internal budget constraint in the Keynesian system; and this internal budget constraint cannot possibly restrict the system to long-run states.

Now the Keynesian system lacks the new aspect to behavior that characterizes Model B. This means as we shall also establish in Chapter 9.11, that the Keynesian system's internal budget is relevant only to macroeconomics.

This accounts for the Keynesian system's internal budget constraint, while ensuring that the system is not restricted to long-run states, suppressing the microeconomics of the real part of the Keynesian system.

On the other hand, Model B reflects the new aspect to behavior described in Chapter 1.4. This accounts for the system's internal budget constraint ensuring that the system is not restricted to long-run states. As well, Model B's internal budget constraint accounts for the system being wholly microeconomic in character.

We shall go further into the Keynesian system in Chapters 8 and 9. We shall discuss in detail in these chapters how Model B and the Keynesian system are both rid of Model A's incorrect form of Say's Law that restricts the system to long-run states. However, we rid Model B of Model A's incorrect Say's Law through microeconomic analysis.

This is by our resolving through Model B, the inconsistency of Model A. This is by bringing the new aspect to behavior described in Chapter 1.4 into Model B. This accounts for Model B unlike the Keynesian system being wholly microeconomic in character.

Keynes, however, rid his system of Model A's incorrect form of Say's Law using macroeconomic analysis. This is through Keynes allowing the aggregate demand and supply of commodities in his system to diverge which rids his system of Model A's incorrect Say's Law.

This means as we discussed in the preface that Keynes' macroeconomics is, as it were, a short-cut to ridding his system of Model A's form of Say's Law. This, however, is a short-cut that is forced on the Keynesian system. Let us review why this is the case.

Through Model B we resolve the inconsistency of Model A; and in so doing we bring a more general approach to microeconomics into Model B compared to the orthodox approach of Model A. This more general approach to microeconomics allows us to rid Model B of Model A's Say's Law.

Hence through Model B we avoid Keynes' macroeconomic short-cut to ridding his system of Model A's Say's Law. This short-cut accounts for the microeconomics of the real part of the Keynesian system being suppressed.

On the other hand, we rid Model B of Model A's Say's Law through microeconomic analysis. This accounts for Model B being wholly microeconomic in character.

In sum, we rid Model B of Model A's Say's Law while preserving Model B as a wholly microeconomic system. On the other hand, Keynes rid his system of Model A's Say's Law in a manner that accounts for the microeconomics of the real part of his system being suppressed.

1.9 Bringing The New Aspect To Behavior Into The Revised Classical System

We have set out in Section 1.4 the new aspect to behavior that will characterize Model B, our revised classical system. This aspect to behavior, to review, is reflected in our taking individuals and firms to be aware that their resources are limited. Hence in determining their demands and supplies, they act in light of this awareness.

There are two facets to this behavior. First, it implies that individuals and firms are aware that their resources are limited. Second, in being aware that their resources are limited, they act in light of this awareness.

This is through individuals and firms determining quantities of commodities demanded and supplied that each sum to their limited resources. Let us discuss how we shall capture in Model B, the overall behavior that we described in Chapter 1.4. This will require capturing both facets to this behavior.

To review, the first facet to this behavior is reflected in individuals and firms being aware that their resources are limited. However, turning first to Model A, we shall find that W, the system's limited flow of resources, is imposed on the system from outside the system by Say's Law.

Hence these resources are outside the behavioral content of the system. As a result, these resources cannot possibly be the means whereby individuals and firms in Model A are made aware that their resources are limited. In contrast, Model B's limited flow of resources W will enter the behavioral content of the system.

This will be the means whereby individuals and firms in the latter system are made aware that their resources are limited. This is how we shall capture in Model B, the first facet to the behavior we have described in Section 1.4.

We next need to capture the second facet to this behavior in Model B. This is that individuals and firms, in being aware that their resources are limited, act in light of this awareness. This will be accomplished in the following way.

We shall examine the orthodox classical system, Model A, to isolate how it is made consistent with limitation in resources. This analysis will be carried out in detail in Chapter 5.6; and it will provide us with a clue as to how we may form Model B's demand and supply functions. Let us, however, now provide a sketch of this analysis.

1.10 How Model A Is Made Consistent With Limitation In Resources

We shall establish in Chapter 5.6 that Model A is made consistent with limitation in resources as a result of the quantities of commodities demanded and supplied being transformed into *relative* quantities demanded and *relative* quantities supplied.

Hence these quantities, in being relative quantities, will each adjust in a relative manner to always sum to Model A's limited resources. This ensures consistency of the system with limitation in resources.

However, we shall also find in Chapter 5.6 that the quantities of commodities demanded (supplied) are transformed in Model A into relative quantities demanded (supplied) as a result of the system being made consistent by the system's incorrect.

This confirms that consistency of Model A with limited resources is ensured as a result of Say's Law being imposed on the system.

In contrast, Model B's functions and hence the behavior or economic rationale of the system will transform the quantities of commodities demanded (supplied) in this system into relative quantities demanded (supplied).

As a result, these quantities in being relative quantities, will also adjust in a relative manner to always sum to Model B's limited resources. This is how we shall capture in Model B the second facet to the behavior that we described in Section 1.4.

That is, how individuals and firms, in being aware that their resources are limited, act in light of this awareness. This is through individuals and firms determining quantities of commodities demanded and supplied that exhaust their resources.

Hence Model B's functions will reflect both facets to the behavior that we described in Section 1.4; since the first facet to this behavior, as discussed in the previous section, has already been captured in the system.

This will mean that Model B in capturing the overall behavior described in Section 1.4 is made consistent with limitation in resources by the behavior or economic rationale of the system. As a result, Model B will reflect the general economic logic that should underlie all price systems.

On the other hand as we discussed, Model A is made consistent with limited resources as a result of Say's Law being imposed on the system. Hence the general economic logic of price systems is suppressed in Model A. This brings inconsistency into the system.

Model A's inconsistency, however, will be resolved through Model B; since consistency with limited resources will be ensured in Model B by the behavior or economic rationale of the system. This will ensure that Model B, unlike Model A, reflects the general economic logic that should underlie all price systems.

1.11 Ensuring Consistency Of Orthodox Price Systems

Let us review the orthodox rules for consistency of price systems. These rules are centered on the need to ensure equality between the number of independent equations and the number of unknowns of a system. That is, to ensure that the counting rule referred to in Section 1.1 is met.

There are, as economists have pointed out various qualifications to the counting rule. [2] Economists, however, frequently simply take equality between the number of independent equations and unknowns of a system to mean that it is reasonable to assume that the system is consistent.

This is in the sense that one set of variables can simultaneously satisfy every equation of the system. Moreover, it is also usually assumed that only one such set of variables exists.

Now while all price systems must meet the counting rule in order to be consistent, we shall find that this rule occupies quite a different place in Model B, our revised classical system, compared to Model A, the orthodox classical system.

This is because while it is a requirement or condition to be met by all systems, meeting this condition in Model B will be a consequence of the general economic consistency of the system. Hence it is not a rule to be imposed on Model B since it is ensured by the behavior or economic rationale of the system.

In contrast, we shall find that Model A meets the counting rule not as a result of consistency of the system's behavior or

---

[2] See, for example, William S. Vickrey, *Microstatics* (New York, 1964), see pages 121-22.

economic rationale. Instead, the counting rule is imposed on Model A from the outside by the Say's Law.

This is an inconsistency since the counting rule should not be imposed on the system by the non-behavioral Say's Law. Instead, Model A should meet the counting rule as a result of the behavior of the system. This will be the case with Model B.

1.12 How The Inconsistency Of Model A Will Be Resolved

We shall resolve the inconsistency we have uncovered in Model A, the orthodox classical system, in the following way. This is through forming a revised classical system, Model B.

This latter system will reflect behavior that ensures consistency of the system with limitation in resources; and we described this behavior in Section 1.4 of the chapter. This, to review, is behavior that is reflected in individuals and firms being aware that their resources are limited.

Hence in determining their commodity demands and supplies, they will act in light of this awareness. This is through individuals and firms determining quantities of commodities demanded (supplied) that exhaust their resources. We also sketched how Model B's functions will capture this behavior.

This will be reflected in Model B's functions first capturing how individuals and firms are aware that their resources are limited. Model B's functions will then determine relative quantities of commodities demanded (supplied).

As a result these quantities, in being relative quantities, will adjust in a relative manner to always sum to Model B's limited resources. This reflects how Model B will capture how individuals and firms act in light of their awareness that their resources are limited.

This is through individuals and firms determining relative quantities of commodities demanded (supplied). Hence they determine quantities that adjust in a relative manner to always sum to their limited resources. Consequently, Model B will capture both facets to the behavior that we described in Section 1.4 of this chapter.

This will result in consistency of the system with limitation in resources being ensured by the behavior or economic rationale of the system. This means that Model B, unlike Model A, will capture the general economic logic of price systems.

As a result, through Model B we shall resolve Model A's economic inconsistency; since this inconsistency, to review, results from Model A being made consistent with limited resources by the non-behavioral Say's Law rather than by the behavior in the system.

Finally, later in the book, in Chapter 7.6, when we can draw on formal versions of Model A and Model B, we shall be able to go further into how through Model B we resolve the inconsistency of Model A. Let us provide a sketch of this analysis.

Model A's inconsistency arose because of an inconsistency in the system's behavioral content. This is because the new aspect to behavior described in Chapter 1.4 is missing from the system.

Hence we have to bring this aspect to behavior into Model A's behavioral content, that is, into the system's demand and supply functions, in order to rid the system of its inconsistency.

This will be accomplished through Model B by our bringing the new set of behavioral functions referred to in the previous section, and hence the new aspect to behavior described in Section 1.4 into this system.

This will account for our resolving through Model B the inconsistency of Model A. However, the new set of behavioral functions to which we have referred is missing from Model A. Hence the inconsistency in the system's behavioral content remains.

1.13 Summary

We described in a general way in this chapter the inconsistency that we have uncovered in the orthodox classical price system, a system we represent by Model A. This system is inconsistent in an economic sense because it lacks an aspect to the behavior of individuals and firms.

This is the aspect to behavior that should ensure that Model A is consistent with limited resources. That is, the aspect to behavior that should ensure that the quantities of commodities demanded (supplied) each sum to the system's limited resources to hence exhaust these resources.

Next, since Model A lacks this aspect to behavior, the system is made consistent with limited resources as a result of Say's Law being imposed on the system to eliminate a surplus equation. We shall, however, resolve Model A's inconsistency through Model B, our revised classical system.

This is because consistency of the latter system with limited resources will be ensured by the behavior or economic rationale of the system rather than by Say's Law as in Model A.

We also introduced the variable W in Section 1.6 of this chapter, a variable which reflects the overall output or income of both Model A and Model B as well as the systems' limited flow of resources. However, despite this similarity between the systems there is a key difference between them as was discussed in Section 1.7.

This is reflected in Model A being characterized by an incorrect form of Say's Law that restricts the system to long-run states. However, the new aspect to behavior of Model B rids this system of Model A's incorrect Say's Law. Yet Model B will reflect Say's Law but a correct form of the Law that cannot possibly restrict this system to long-run states.

Next, as discussed in the chapter, Model A and Model B are both long-run microeconomic systems that are characterized by the identical variable W that reflects the limited flow of resources of both systems.

Yet Model B will have a more general character than Model A. This is because we shall bring into Model B the new aspect to behavior described in Section 1.4 of the chapter. On the other hand, this aspect to behavior is suppressed in Model A.

We shall also discuss in Chapters 2.5 and 2.6 how we shall approach budget constraints in this book by dealing with the limited resources that give rise to these budget constraints.

This means that we may also refer to the new aspect to behavior of our new systems in the following way: this new aspect to behavior is reflected in our taking individuals and firms to be aware that they are subject to a budget constraint.

Hence in determining their commodity demands and supplies, they act in light of this awareness. This is through individuals and firms determining quantities of commodities demanded and supplied that always exhaust their budget constraints.

Chapter 2

Remarks On The Inconsistency In The Orthodox Classical Price System

2.1 Introduction

We described in the previous chapter the inconsistency that we have uncovered in the orthodox classical system, Model A. This inconsistency arises because this system does not reflect the general economic logic that should underlie all price systems.

This is because the behavior or economic rationale of Model A does not ensure that the system is consistent with limitation in resources. Instead, Model A is made consistent with limitation in resources as a result of Say's Law being imposed on the system to eliminate a surplus equation.

Model A's inconsistency, however, will be resolved through Model B; since consistency of the latter system with limitation in resources will be ensured by the system's behavior or economic rationale. This will result in Model B, unlike Model A, reflecting the general economic logic that should underlie all price systems.

We shall also discuss in Sections 2.5 and 2.6 of the chapter how we deal in this book with budget constraints in a more satisfactory manner compared to how they are dealt with in orthodox analysis. Then in Section 2.7 we shall go into detail concerning Model B's internal budget constraint.

Next, in Section 2.8 we shall bring out some basic issues with the Keynesian system, issues that will be covered more fully in Chapter 9; and in Section 2.9 we shall contrast how consistency of Model A and Model B is ensured.

Then Section 2.10, we shall review how we approach Say's Law in the book; and in Section 2.11 we shall discuss why the inconsistency of Model A remained hidden.

Finally, on the basis of the analyses of Chapter 1 and the present chapter we shall provide a sketch in Chapter 2.12 of the overall rationale of the book. However, we shall review this analysis in Chapter 6 in the content of the formal versions of Model A and Model B that will then be available.

2.2 Remarks On Ensuring Consistency Of Price Systems

Model A is initially inconsistent in an economic sense because the system's behavior, and hence the system's demand and supply functions, do not ensure that the system is consistent with limitation in resources.

That is, Model A's functions do not capture the general economic logic that should characterize all price systems. This is then reflected in the number of independent equations and unknowns in the system not being equal.

Economists then proceed to ensure that the system is consistent. This is usually done by imposing Say's Law on the system to eliminate a surplus equation to make the system consistent. That is, to ensure that the system meets the counting rule.

However, this is a misuse of the Law which as discussed in Chapter 1.3 results in an incorrect or misused form of the Law being imposed on Model A. This incorrect or misused Say's Law then ensures that Model A is consistent with limitation in resources.

This approach, however, gives a role to Model A's Say's Law that is properly a role for the system's economics. This is the role of ensuring that Model A is consistent with limitation in resources.

This leads to Say's Law being given precedence over economic consistency in ensuring that Model A is consistent with limitation in resources. However, Model B's demand and supply functions will reflect behavior that ensures consistency of the system with limitation in resources.

Hence we shall remove from Model B the incorrect role that Say's Law plays in Model A of ensuring consistency of the latter system with limitation in resources. This will be confirmed in the following way.

We shall find, as will be discussed in Chapter 6.4, that Model B is automatically consistent. That is, the number of independent equations and the number of unknowns in the system are automatically equal.

This means that we rid Model B of the role of Model A's incorrect Say's Law of ensuring that the latter system is

consistent. This will account for Model B having a more general
character than Model A.

2.3 Details Of The Inconsistency In The Orthodox
Classical System

We discussed the inconsistency of Model A and how it will be
resolved in Chapters 1.3 and 1.12 respectively. However, we shall
find it useful to provide more details concerning these analyses.
This discussion will also bring up the relevance of Say's Law to
this inconsistency.

Model A's inconsistency arises because the system's
behavior does not ensure consistency of the system with
limitation in resources. That is, Model A does not capture the
general economic logic that should underlie all price systems.

This is because Model A lacks the aspect to behavior that
we described in Chapter 1.4. This is the aspect to behavior that
should ensure consistency of the system with limited resources.
This creates a gap in the behavioral content of the system.

We shall, however, bring this aspect to behavior that is
missing from Model A into Model B. Hence through the latter
system, we shall resolve the inconsistency of Model A.

This aspect to behavior, to review, is reflected in us taking
individuals and firms in Model B to be aware that their resources
are limited. Hence in determining their demands and supplies,
they act in light of this awareness.

Moreover, individuals and firms in Model B will act in
light of their awareness that their resources are limited by
determining relative quantities of commodities demanded
(supplied).

Hence these quantities in being relative quantities adjust
in a relative manner to always exhaust the system's limited
resources. This is the second facet to the behavior described in
Chapter 1.4. Let us now consider Model A.

Drawing on the analysis of Chapter 1.10, consistency of
price systems with limitation in resources must be ensured by the
quantities of commodities demanded (supplied) being transformed
into relative quantities demanded (supplied).

This is because these quantities, in being relative
quantities, will adjust in a relative manner to always sum to the
systems' limited resources. Model A's functions, however, initially

determine absolute rather than relative quantities of commodities demanded (supplied).

Hence the system is initially inconsistent with limitation in resources since the quantities of commodities demanded (supplied) will not necessarily sum to the system's limited resources. This causes Model A to be initially inconsistent in being characterized by a surplus equation over the number of unknowns.

Economists then usually impose Say's Law on Model A to eliminate a surplus equation to make the system consistent. This ensures that Model A is consistent with limitation in resources.

This as we discussed in Chapter 1.10 is by the quantities of commodities demanded (supplied) being transformed into relative quantities demanded (supplied) as a result of the system being made consistent by Say's Law.

Hence the quantities demanded (supplied) in Model A, in being relative quantities, will adjust in a relative manner to always sum to the system's limited resources. This ensures consistency of Model A with limitation in resources. Yet the system remains inconsistent.

This is because consistency of Model A with limitation in resources should be ensured by the behavior in the system. Instead, consistency of Model A with limited resources is ensured as a result of Say's Law being imposed on the system to eliminate a surplus equation.

This is because Model A lacks the new aspect to behavior described in Chapter 1.4 that should ensure that the system is consistent with limitation in resources. We shall now discuss how this new aspect to behavior will be formally brought into Model B's demand and supply functions.

2.4 Model B's Interior Or Internal Functions

We shall put additional functions, to be called interior or internal functions, into Model B's demand and supply functions. These interior functions, as we shall now discuss, will account for Model B's demand and supply functions bringing the new aspect to behavior described in Chapter 1.4 into the system.

Model B's interior functions will make the ratios of the quantities of commodities demanded, and the ratios of the quantities of commodities supplied, depend on the relative prices.

Hence these interior or internal functions, in determining only the ratios of the quantities demanded (supplied) cannot, on their own, determine the quantities of commodities demanded and supplied.

These interior functions of Model B can only determine the quantities of commodities demanded (supplied) by operating on W, the system's limited flow of resources. However, these interior functions are within Model B's demand (supply) functions.

As a result, these interior functions will bring the variable W that reflects the limited flow of resources of both Model A and Model B from outside the behavioral content of Model A into Model B's demand and supply functions. That is, into the behavioral content of Model B.

This is how individuals and firms in Model B are made aware that their resources are limited. Next, individuals and firms will act in light of their awareness that their resources are limited.

This is through individuals and firms determining quantities of commodities demanded (supplied) that exhaust their limited resources. Moreover, this is also ensured by Model B's interior functions.

This is on account of these functions operating on the system's limited resources to determine relative quantities of commodities demanded (supplied). Hence the quantities demanded (supplied) in Model B, in being relative quantities, will adjust in a relative manner to always sum to Model B's limited resources.

Consequently, Model B will reflect the overall aspect to behavior described in Chapter 1.4. This is because we capture both facets to this behavior in the system. Whereas this behavior is missing from Model A which accounts for the inconsistency we have uncovered in this system.

2.5 Dealing In A More General Manner With The Budget Constraints Of Price Systems

We shall arrive at a more satisfactory approach to price systems by dealing in a more general way with the budget constraints of price systems compared to how they are dealt with in orthodox price systems.

Budget constraints arise as a result of limitation in resources in price systems. Next, in Chapter 1.6 we isolated the variable W that reflects the limited flow of resources of both

Model A and Model B. We shall now bring out how our approach to budget constraints differs from the orthodox approach.

Budget constraints are imposed on orthodox microeconomic price systems such as Model A. Hence these external budget constraints impose a limited flow of resources on the systems. These budget constraints, however, restrict the generality of the systems.

This is reflected, for example, in Model A's external budget constraint form of Say's Law restricting the system to long-run states. We shall, however, adopt a more general approach to the budget constraints of our new systems, systems we represent by Model B.

This approach is reflected in us dealing with the budget constraints of our new systems by dealing with the variable W which reflects the limited flow of resources of the systems. Hence since W is the basis of the systems' budget constraints, we shall in dealing with W bring budget constraints into our new systems.

Moreover, these budget constraints will be more general that the externally-imposed budget constraints of orthodox systems. This is because they will be determined internally in our new systems hence they cannot possibly restrict the systems to any particular states.

On the other hand, budget constraints are imposed on orthodox microeconomic price systems such as Model A. Hence these external budget constraints impose a limited flow of resources on the systems; and these budget constraints restrict the generality of the systems.

This, to review, is reflected in Model A's external budget constraint restricting this system to long-run states. This is because Model A does not deal with its budget constraint in the more general manner described whereby we deal with the budget constraints of our new systems, systems we represent by Model B.

2.6 Remarks On Limitation In Resources And The Budget Constraints Of Price Systems

Budget constraints are imposed on orthodox systems such as Model A. Hence these are external budget constraints which impose a limited volume of resources on the systems to cause these budget constraints to restrict the systems to particular states.

This is reflected in Model A's external budget constraint form of Say's Law restricting the system to long-run states.

However, we shall avoid this problem by transforming the external budget constraints of orthodox systems into internal budget constraints in our new systems, systems we represent by Model B.

Now all price systems are necessarily subject to limitation in resources. This is usually captured in orthodox price theory through an assumption that orthodox systems are characterized by some given or fixed volume of resources.

There is a counterpart to this assumption in our analysis which is reflected in the imposing of the variable W by Say's Law on Model A. This variable as we discussed in Chapter 1.6 reflects the limited flow of resources of both Model A and Model B. There is, however, a basic difference between the systems.

As discussed, the limited flow of resources W is imposed on Model A from the outside by Say's Law. Hence these resources remain outside the system's behavioral content.

These resources in being outside the system's behavioral content then form the basis for an external budget constraint. This we shall find is an incorrect form of Say's Law that restricts Model A to long-run states. Let us now consider Model B.

We assume that individuals and firms in Model B will be aware that their resources are limited. This assumption is made because individuals and firms in determining their commodity demands and supplies will be constrained by these resources.

This necessarily implies that they will be aware that their resources are limited. This explains why we assume in this book that individuals and firms in Model B are aware that their resources are limited.

Next, we can only ensure that individuals and firms in Model B are aware that their resources are limited by these resources being brought into the behavioral content of the system. That is into the system's demand and supply functions.

These resources, in being within Model B's behavioral content, then become the means whereby individuals and firms are made aware that their resources are limited.

These resources in being within Model B's behavioral content then form the basis for an internal budget constraint in the system. This internal budget constraint we shall find reflects a correct form of Say's Law in being a true identity that cannot possibly restrict Model B to long-run states.

This analysis brings out the key role of our assumption that individuals and firms in Model B are aware that their resources are limited.

Now the variable W is put outside the behavioral content of Model A by the system's incorrect Say's Law. This is a form of the Law that is an external budget constraint that restricts the system to long-run states.

However, our assumption that individuals and firms in Model B are aware that their resources are limited brings W from outside the behavioral content of Model A into the behavioral content of Model B.

This rids Model B of Model A's Say's Law that accounts for W being put outside the latter system's behavioral content and which restricts the system to long-run states. This is replaced in Model B with a correct form of the Law that is an internal budget constraint that cannot possibly restrict the latter system to long-run states.

We emphasize that Model B remains characterized by the identical variable W that is imposed on Model A by Say's Law. However, W moves into the behavioral content of Model B on account of our assumption that individuals and firms are aware that their resources are limited.

Now W forms the basis for a budget constraint in Model A; and W must also necessarily form the basis for a budget constraint in Model B. However, since W is outside the behavioral content of Model A it cannot possibly be made the basis for a budget constraint by the behavior in the system.

This explains why the W of Model A is made the basis for a budget constraint in Model A by the non-behavioral Say's Law. This is through the Law, in ensuring consistency of Model A, ensuring that the quantities of commodities demanded (supplied) each sum to W. This accounts for W providing the basis for Model A's budget constraint.

This whole process, however, operates outside Model A's behavioral content to explain why this system is subject to an externally-imposed budget constraint. Let us now consider Model B.

We have discussed how W moves from outside the behavioral content of Model A into the behavioral content of Model B. Moreover, W must also form the basis for a budget constraint in this system.

However, since W is within Model B's behavioral content it must be made the basis for a budget constraint by the behavior in the system. Were this not the case W would move back to being outside the behavioral content of Model A to form the basis for the system's external budget constraint.

We can now bring out the significance of Model B's internal or interior functions that we discussed in Section 2.4 of this chapter. These behavioral functions exist within the behavior content of Model B.

They then operate on the system's W that is also within the system's behavioral content to determine quantities of commodities demanded (supplied) that each necessarily sum to W.

Hence the W of Model B is made the basis for a budget constraint in the system on account of the behavior in the system. This reflects how W forms the basis for an internal budget constraint in Model B, a budget constraint that cannot possibly restrict the system to long-run states.

We emphasize that both Model A and Model B are long-run systems. However, Model A is necessarily restricted to long-run states by the system's externally-imposed budget constraint.

In contrast, while Model B also describes long-run states, it is not restricted to such states by Model A's external budget constraint which is an incorrect form of Say's Law.

Instead, Model B is characterized by an internal budget constraint that reflects a correct form of Say's Law that cannot possibly restrict this system to long-run states.

Finally, this analysis brings out from the perspective of budget constraints how we resolve the inconsistency of Model A through Model B. This inconsistency, to review, is reflected in consistency with limitation in resources being ensured in Model A as a result of Say's Law being imposed on the system to eliminate a surplus equation.

However, this inconsistency is resolved through Model B since consistency of this system with limitation in resource is ensured through the behavior in the system.

Next, consistency of price systems with limitation in resources is ensured through the systems' budget constraints. Hence we would expect that Model B's budget constraint is also determined by the behavior in the system. This will be confirmed in detail later in the book, see Chapter 6.15. Let us now consider Model A.

Inconsistency enters Model A because consistency of the system with limitation in resources is not ensured by the behavior in the system but is ensured instead as a result of Say's Law being imposed on the system.

Hence we would also expect that Model A's budget constraint is not ensured by the behavior in the system but is ensured as a result of the system being made consistent by Say's

Law. This will also be confirmed in detail later in the book in Chapter 6.15.

2.7 Model B's Internal Budget Constraint

We discussed in Section 2.5 how we shall bring internal budget constraints into our new systems by dealing with the limited flow of resources that gives rise to these budget constraints. Let us now focus specifically on Model B's internal budget constraint.

Model B's limited flow of resources is reflected in the variable W which also reflects the system's overall output or income.

Next, the new aspect to behavior of Model B brings W into the system's behavioral content where it forms the basis for an internal budget constraint. This internal budget constraint as we shall now establish is a true identity form of Say's Law.

Model B's internal functions described in Chapter 2.4 determine the ratios of the quantities of commodities demanded and the ratios of the quantities of commodities supplied respectively.

Next, as will be discussed in more detail in Chapter 6.3 one set of these internal functions will operate on the W of Model B to determine relative quantities of commodities demanded. Hence the quantities demanded in being relative quantities will adjust in a relative manner to always sum to W.

Then as will also be discussed in Chapter 6.3, another set of these internal functions will operate on the W of Model B to determine relative quantities of quantities of commodities supplied. Hence the quantities supplied in being relative quantities will also adjust in a relative manner to always sum to the variable W.

Now when we say that one set of Model B's interior functions operate on W to determine quantities demanded that sum to W we were taking or describing W as the aggregate demand for commodities.

Then when we say that another set of the interior functions of Model B operate on W to determine quantities supplied that sum to W we were now taking or describing W as the aggregate supply of commodities.

Consequently, Model B is characterized by Say's Law since the system's interior functions allow us to describe the system's overall output or income W alternately as aggregate demand and aggregate supply. This is a correct identity form of the Law since it is solely a descriptive device in Model B.

Moreover, individual quantities of commodities demanded (supplied) emerge from this correct identity form of the Law which ensures that Model B is wholly microeconomic in character.

This accounts for Model B, as we shall discuss in detail in Chapter 9.7 being characterized by a correct form of Say's Law. This we shall find is a true identity that also acts as a budget constraint of relevance to microeconomics in a system. Finally, we shall formally set out Model B's internal budget constraint in Chapter 6.5.

2.8 Issues Concerning The Keynesian System

Keynes held that Model A is restricted to long-run states by Say's Law. However, we shall establish that while Model A is indeed restricted to long-run states, this is because the system is characterized by an incorrect or misused form of the Law; and it is this incorrect Say's Law that restricts Model A to long-run states.

Now economists in setting out Model A write Say's Law as an identity. However, this identity is misused in Model A in being given the substantive role in Model A of eliminating a surplus equation to ensure consistency of the system.

This explains why we concluded that there is an incorrect or misused form of the Law in Model A; since a correct form of the Law should not be given the substantive role described.

We recognize in this book that Model A is characterized by an incorrect form of Say's Law that accounts for the system being restricted to long-run states. Hence the solution to this is to bring a correct form of the Law into Model A. Keynes, however, did not follow this approach.

Instead, Keynes wholly removed Model A's incorrect Say's Law from his system. This was through Keynes allowing the aggregate demand and supply of commodities in his system to diverge. Let us discuss the consequences of this for the Keynesian system.

There are two properties that stem from Model A's incorrect Say's Law. First, it restricts Model A to long-run states. Second, it forms the basis for a budget constraint of relevance to microeconomics. This is because individual quantities of commodities demanded (supplied) emerge from this budget constraint. This accounts for Model A being wholly microeconomic in character.

Hence Keynes in wholly ridding his system of Model A's incorrect Say's Law, rid his system of both of the properties that we described stem from Model A's Say's Law.

Consequently, the Keynesian system, in being rid of the first property of Model A's incorrect Say's Law, can move to alternative states as behavior changes; since the system is not restricted to long-run states by Model A's incorrect Say's Law.

Keynes, however, simultaneously rid his system of the second property of Model A's incorrect Say's Law. This is the property that is reflected in Say's Law providing the basis in Model A for a budget constraint of relevance to microeconomics.

Keynes' ridding his system of this second property of Model A's incorrect Say's Law then accounts for the microeconomics of the real part of his system being suppressed. Let us now consider Model B.

We rid Model B of Model A's incorrect Say's Law by our transforming this incorrect Say's Law from being an externally-imposed budget constraint into an internal budget constraint in Model B.

This internal budget constraint first replaces Model A's incorrect Say's Law which is not a true identity with a true identity form of the Law in Model B. Hence Model B like the Keynesian system, is not restricted to long-run states by Model A's incorrect Say's Law.

However, we do not rid Model B of the second property of Model A's incorrect Say's Law. This is the property reflected in Model A's incorrect Say's Law providing the basis for a budget constraint of relevance to microeconomics in the system.

Instead, we bring this property correctly into Model B through this system's internal budget constraint. This is because this internal budget constraint accounts for a budget constraint of relevance to microeconomics entering Model B on account of the behavior in the system.

Whereas Model A's budget constraint that is also of relevance to microeconomics enters the system as a result of the non-behavioral Say's Law being imposed on the system.

Hence to summarize the preceding analyses, Keynes did not rid his system of Model A's incorrect Say's Law in a satisfactory manner; since this is accomplished in a manner that accounts for the microeconomics of the real part of the Keynesian system being suppressed.

On the other hand, we rid Model B of Model A's incorrect Say's Law in a manner that ensures that Model B is wholly microeconomic in character. We shall discuss the findings of this section in fuller detail in Chapter 9.

Finally, the preceding analyses will assist us later in the book in bringing out a basic issue with how Keynes approached the classical system and Say's Law.

Now the orthodox classical system, Model A, is restricted to long-run states by Say's Law, a form of the Law which we established is an incorrect or misused form of the Law.

Keynes, to review, then wholly removed Model A's Say's Law from his system. This means that the Keynesian system is not restricted by the Law to long-run states hence it can move to alternative states as behavior changes, a reflection of the system's macroeconomic character.

However, while Model A's incorrect Say's Law does indeed restrict the system to long-run states the solution to this is not simply to rid this system of this incorrect form of the Law.

We need to ask the question of why, in the first place, an incorrect form of the Law entered Model A? Through pursuing this question, we uncover that an incorrect form of Say's Law enters Model A because of the inconsistency we uncover in the system.

This inconsistency arose because Model A lacks the new aspect to behavior described in Chapter 1.4. However, we bring this new aspect behavior into Model B. Hence through the latter system, we resolve the inconsistency of Model A.

This accounts for Model B being rid of Model A's incorrect Say's Law in a manner that ensures that Model B is wholly microeconomic in character.

On the other hand, Keynes rid his system of Model A's Say's Law in a manner that results in the microeconomics of the real part of the Keynesian system being suppressed. The issues raised in this section will be covered in fuller detail later in the book see, for example, Chapter 9.

2.9 Contrasting How Consistency Of Model A And Model B Is Ensured

We have discussed how consistency is imposed on Model A through the imposing of the counting rule on the system. This is accomplished through an incorrect form of Say's Law being imposed on the system to eliminate a surplus equation. This incorrect Say's Law then restricts Model A to long-run states.

We need, of course, to ensure that price systems meet the counting rule. However, we need to apply this rule to Model A in a manner that does not result in the system being restricted to long-run states. This will be accomplished in the following way.

We showed that Say's Law in being imposed on Model A, ensures that the system is consistent with limitation in resources. This is an approach that which brings inconsistency into the system; since consistency of Model A with limitation in resources should be ensured by the behavior in the system.

This means that if we could find a behavioral means to ensure consistency of Model A with limited resources, we would avoid having to impose consistency on the system through Say's Law to hence avoid the system's inconsistency.

Nonetheless, this alternative behavioral approach to ensuring consistency of Model A with limitation in resources would yet have to ensure consistency of the system in the following sense. That is, it would also have to ensure that the number of independent equations and unknowns are equal as called for by the counting rule.

We shall establish that this behavioral substitute for the counting rule is the new aspect to behavior described in Chapter 1.4 that we bring into Model B. This means that this new aspect to behavior ensures consistency of Model B with limited resources.

Moreover, as will be discussed in Chapter 6.4, it also ensures consistency of Model B in the sense of ensuring equality of the number of independent equations and unknowns in the system. Hence through this new aspect to behavior that we bring into Model B, we found a behavioral means of ensuring consistency of Model B.

As a result, we do not have to *impose* the counting rule on Model B through Say's Law as has to be done in the case of Model A; since the behavior in Model B ensures that the system meets the counting rule.

This difference between the systems accounts for Model A being restricted to long-run states by an incorrect form of Say's Law. On the other hand, Model B is not restricted by such an incorrect Say's Law to long-run states.

2.10 Approaching The Issue Of Say's Law Restricting Model A To Long-Run States

Say's Law is a non-behavioral element that is imposed on Model A to eliminate a surplus equation to ensure consistency of the system. This as we established accounts for the system being characterized by an incorrect or misused form of the Law that restricts the system to long-run states.

However, we cannot simply remove the Law from the system; since we would return to Model A in its initial state where it is characterized by a surplus equation over the number of unknowns.

We have to rid Model A of its incorrect form of the Law by finding a behavioral substitute for this incorrect Law. Let us sketch how this will be accomplished. Now the Law not only rids Model A of a surplus equation.

We also establish that the Law suppresses an aspect to the behavior of individuals and firms in the system. This is the aspect to behavior that should ensure consistency of Model A with limitation in resources.

We shall then resolve this inconsistency of Model A through Model B by bringing the new aspect to behavior described in Chapter 1.4 into the latter system. This means that the Law in Model B is rid of the invalid role imputed to the Law in Model A of ensuring consistency of the latter system with limitation in resources.

This accounts for Model B being rid of Model A's incorrect form of the Law that restricts the latter system to long-run states. This will be confirmed by Model B being characterized by a correct identity form of the Law that cannot possibly restrict the system to long-run states.

This is because as we established in Section 2.7 and will confirm in Chapter 6.3, the Law in Model B is solely a descriptive device in this system. Let us summarize this analysis in the following way.

We remove in Model B the incorrect role that Say's Law plays in Model A of ensuring consistency of the latter system with limitation in resources; and we give this role to the behavior of Model B.

This accounts for consistency of Model B with limitation in resources being ensured by the behavior in the system rather than by Say's Law as in Model A. This means that Model B reflects the general economic logic of price systems whereas this logic is suppressed in Model A.

2.11 Why The Inconsistency Of Model A Remained Hidden

Model A, to review, is subject to an economic inconsistency. This is because the system's demand and supply functions, and hence the behavior or economic rationale of the system, does not ensure that the system is consistent with limitation in resources.

That is, Model A's functions do not ensure that the quantities of commodities demanded (supplied) each sum to the system's limited resources to exhaust these resources. This results in Model A being initially inconsistent in that the number of independent equations and unknowns are not initially equal.

Economists then usually proceed to ensure consistency of the system by imposing Say's Law on the system to eliminate the system's equation; and this ensures that the system is consistent with limitation in resources. Say's Law is misused in Model A.

This is because the system's initial inconsistency is the result of an economic inconsistency. As a result, making Model A consistent by imposing Say's Law on the system implies using the non-behavioral Law to resolve an economic inconsistency in the system, which is impossible.

Consequently, Model A remains inconsistent in an economic sense; since while the system reflects consistency with limited resources, this is not ensured by the behavior in the system. This economic inconsistency, however, remained hidden.

This is because the system's economic inconsistency is reflected in the system being inconsistent in being characterized by a surplus equation. Economists then ensure that Model A is consistent by using Say's Law to eliminate the system's surplus equation leading them to conclude that the system is consistent.

This means that the whole issue of how the general economic consistency of Model A should be ensured shifted into the background. This is the issue of ensuring that consistency of the system with limited resources be ensured by the behavior in the system.

This is because Model A seems indeed to be consistent in being consistent in the sense that the number of independent equations and the number of unknowns in the system are equal.

However, the system was deemed to be consistent on the basis of being consistent in this sense rather than in an economic sense. This is because while Model A is consistent in meeting the

counting rule, hidden within the system is the economic
inconsistency we have described.

This, to review, is reflected in consistency of the system
with limitation in resources being ensured as a result of Say's
Law being imposed on the system rather than being ensured by
the behavior in the system. Let us sketch how this will be
resolved.

We shall revise Model A, through Model B, by ensuring
that consistency of the latter system with limitation in resources
is ensured by the behavior in the system.

Moreover, this as will be discussed in Chapter 6.4 will also
ensure that Model B is consistent in meeting the counting rule.
Hence consistency of Model B will be a result of the system's
economic consistency.

That is, a result of Model B being made consistent with
limitation in resources by the behavior in the system. This will
resolve the inconsistency of Model A that is reflected in Say's Law
rather than the behavior in the system, ensuring that the system
is consistent with limitation in resources.

2.12 The Overall Rationale Of The Book

Drawing on the analyses of Chapter 1 and the present chapter we
are now in a position to sketch the overall rationale of the book.
However, we shall review this analysis in Chapter 6 in the
content of the formal versions of Model A and Model B that will
then be available.

Model A, the orthodox classical system is initially
inconsistent in that it does not initially meet the counting rule
since there is a surplus equation over the number of unknowns.
Say's Law is then imposed on the system to eliminate a surplus
equation to ensure consistency of the system.

This however, as we discussed earlier results in an
incorrect form of the Law being imposed on the system that
restricts it to long-run states. This is because Model A is made
consistent by the non-behavioral Say's Law rather than by the
behavior in the system.

Now it is Model A's functions and hence the behavior in
the system that causes the system to be initially inconsistent.
This then causes economists to impose Say's Law on the system.

Hence to rid Model A of its incorrect Say's Law we need to
look into the system's behavioral content. That is, into the

system's demand and supply functions. It is in so doing that we came upon the economic inconsistency in Model A.

Next, as we shall now discuss, in resolving Model A's inconsistency through Model B, we rid the latter system of the Say's Law of Model A that restricts the latter system to long-run state.

Say's Law not only ensures consistency of Model A by eliminating a surplus equation from the system. We established in Chapter 1.3 that the Law simultaneously ensures consistency of the system with limitation in resources.

This brought an economic inconsistency into Model A since consistency of the system with limitation in resources should be ensured by the behavior in the system.

However, we resolved this inconsistency of Model A through Model B by bringing the new aspect to behavior described in Chapter 1.4 into the latter system.

This accounts for Model B automatically meeting the counting rule. Hence we do not need the Law to ensure consistency of Model B. Consequently, we rid the latter system of Model A's incorrect Say's Law that restricts this system to long-run states.

This is replaced in Model B with a correct identity form of the Law that cannot possible restrict the latter system to long-run states. This means that Model A is restricted in generality compared to Model B.

Most generally, this is because consistency of Model A is incorrectly ensured in being ensured by the non-behavioral Say's Law. On the other hand, consistency of Model B is correctly ensured in being ensured by the behavior in the system. There is a further stage to our analysis.

As we discussed, through bringing the new aspect to behavior described in Chapter 1.4 into Model B we brought a correct form of the Law into this system. Let establish more precisely how this was accomplished.

Model B's new aspect to behavior brings a correct identity form of the Law into Model B. This is by bringing an internal budget constraint into the system.

This internal budget constraint is a true identity form of the Law hence it cannot restrict Model B to long-run states. In contrast, the new aspect to behavior of Model B is absent from Model A.

This accounts for this latter system being characterized by an external budget constraint. This is not a true identity form of the Law; and it accounts for Model A being restricted to long-run states. In sum, much of the book turns on how consistency of Model A and Model B is ensured.

To review, Say's Law is imposed on Model A to eliminate a surplus equation to ensure that the system meets the counting rule. This very approach, however, brings an economic inconsistency into the system; since it accounts for consistency with limitation in resources being ensured in Model A in a non-behavioral manner rather than by the behavior in the system.

On the other hand, the new aspect to behavior of Model B ensures that the system meets the counting rule. This approach rids Model B of the economic inconsistency of Model A; since it accounts for consistency with limitation in resources being ensured in Model B by the behavior in the system.

Finally, we may confirm that Model B is rid of the inconsistency of Model A in the following way. This is through Model A being characterized by an external budget constraint form of Say's Law which is not a true identity; and this incorrect form of the Law restricts the system to long-run states.

On the other hand, Model B is characterized by an internal budget constraint form of Say's Law which is a true identity; and this correct form of the Law cannot possibly restrict this system to long-run states.

2.13 Summary

We discussed in the previous chapter how Model A, the orthodox classical system, is inconsistent in an economic sense. This inconsistency arises because the behavior or economic rationale of Model A does not ensure that the system is consistent with limitation in resources.

That is, the behavior in Model A does not ensure that the quantities of commodities demanded (supplied) each sum to the system's limited resources to exhaust these resources.

Instead, Model A is made consistent with limitation in resources as a result of the system being made consistent by an incorrect form of Say's Law. This brings inconsistency into Model A since consistency of the system with limitation in resources should be ensured by the system's behavior or economic rationale.

Model A's inconsistency, however, will be resolved through Model B; since consistency of the latter system with limited resources will be ensured by the system's behavior or economic rationale.

This brings the general economic logic that should characterize all price systems into Model B, a logic that is suppressed in Model A. This restricts the generality of the latter system.

We also discussed in Sections 2.5 and 2.6 of the chapter how we deal in this book with budget constraints in a more satisfactory manner compared to how they are dealt with in orthodox analysis.

Then in Section 2.7 we went into detail concerning Model B's internal budget constraint which, as we noted, will be formally set out in Chapter 6.5.

Next, in Section 2.8 we brought out some basic issues with the Keynesian system, issues that will be covered more fully in Chapter 9; and in Section 2.9 we contrasted how consistency of Model A and Model B is ensured.

Then Section 2.10, we reviewed how we approached Say's Law in the book; and in Section 2.11 we discussed why the inconsistency of Model A remained hidden.

Finally, on the basis of the analyses of Chapter 1 and the present chapter we provided a sketch in Chapter 2.12 of the overall rationale of the book. However, we shall review this analysis in Chapter 6 in the context of the formal versions of Model A and Model B that will then be available.

Chapter 3

The Orthodox Classical Price System

3.1 Introduction

We shall now formally set out Model A, the system that we take to reflect the orthodox classical system.[3] There are a number of variants of this system in the literature. However, there is a common element to them in that they are all characterized by what is referred to as an "homogeneity postulate."

This is reflected in the systems' commodity demand and supply functions depending only on the relative commodity prices which are the ratios of the money prices of commodities.

Hence Model A, our version of the orthodox classical system, while differing in some ways from other forms of the system, will also be subject to this postulate; since this postulate is the distinguishing feature of the orthodox classical system. Let us go further into Model A.

We shall take Model A as a market system hence basing it on market demand and supply functions. As well, we shall initially develop it as a real system. Next, we shall discuss how the system is inconsistent in that there is a surplus equation over the number of unknowns.

Model A is then made consistent by Say's Law being imposed on the system to eliminate this surplus equation. However, while generally being taken to be consistent, we shall find that Model A reflects the inconsistency that we have uncovered in the system; and we shall review this inconsistency and sketch how it will be resolved.

We shall then follow the orthodox literature and add a money equation to Model A to determine the system's price level. Patinkin, however, has shown that Model A, which he took as a neoclassical system, is subject to an indeterminate price level and an invalid real-monetary dichotomy. However, we shall establish

---

[3] On this system, see W.B. Hickman, "The Determinacy of Absolute Prices in Classical Economic Theory," *Econometrica,* XVlll (1950), pps. 9-20 and Patinkin, *op. cit.,* Ch. VIII.

in Chapter 10 that the problems with Model A that Patinkin raised are resolved through Model B, our revised form of Model A. Let us provide a sketch of this analysis.

Patinkin has shown that Model A is dichotomized into real and monetary parts which accounts for the system's price level being indeterminate.

He then concluded that this is an invalid dichotomy in that it causes the system's price level to be indeterminate. However, we shall establish in Chapter 10 that the price level of Model B is determinate.

Yet Model B, like Model A, is a dichotomized system since we also solve in Model B for the relative prices independently of the price level. Hence Model B's dichotomy does not cause the system's price level to be indeterminate. This means that Model B, unlike Model A, is characterized by a valid real-monetary dichotomy.

3.2 Orthodox Microeconomic Price Systems

Orthodox microeconomic price systems such as Model A are based on market demand and supply functions that are intended to reflect the economic behavior of individuals and firms.[4]

This is in the sense that the functions show the quantities of commodities demanded and the quantities supplied at various prices, assuming that all other influences on these demands and supplies are fixed. These are the tastes and preferences of individuals and firms as well as their resources.

Moreover, population and the state of technology are held fixed. There is next the question of consistency of the systems. Behavior in the systems must, of course, meet the well-known axioms or conditions for consistency and rationality of behavior set out in the literature.[5]

We also discussed in Chapter 1.11 how economists ensure consistency of orthodox systems such as Model A; and they use a counting rule to ensure such consistency. This is through equating the number of independent equations and unknowns in the systems.

---

[4] See, for example, Hickman, *op. cit.*, pps. 9-20.

[5] On these axioms or conditions for consistency and rationality of behavior see J.M. Henderson and R.E. Quandt, *Microeconomic Theory: A Mathematical Approach* (New York, 1958), Chs. 2 and 3. Also, Vickrey, *op. cit.*, where Ch. 2 considers the consumer and Ch. 4 considers the firm.

There are various qualifications to this counting rule as economists have pointed out. However, we also discussed in Chapter 1.11 how economists frequently simply take equality between the number of independent equations and unknowns of a system to mean that it is reasonable to assume that the system is consistent.

Consistency, when ensured by a system meeting this counting rule, implies that one set of variables can simultaneously satisfy every equation in the system.

As well, we pointed out that economists also usually assume that there exists only one set of variables that simultaneously satisfies every equation of a system. With this as background, let us now focus on the orthodox classical system, Model A.

This is a long-run system; and it will allow us to illustrate the general nature of the orthodox microeconomic price systems considered in this book as well as how consistency of the systems is usually ensured along orthodox lines. Yet we shall find that Model A is characterized by the economic inconsistency that has been uncovered in this book.

3.3 A Preliminary Form Of The Orthodox Classical System

We shall set out Model A by basing it on a preliminary form of the system, Model A', that is shown below. This is a preliminary form of Model A since it will have to be adapted to ensure that it reflects rational behavior:

Model A'

1. $D_j \equiv F(p_j)$

2. $S_j \equiv G(p_j)$

3. $E(p_j) = 0$

Model A' is a system in which there are n commodities. There is also a fixed supply of outside money which is assumed to be a neutral medium-of-exchange. Hence we define commodities to exclude money.

We use the variables D_j and S_j to denote the quantities of commodities demanded and supplied, respectively, $j=1,2,3,...,n$. There are also n money prices of commodities, denoted by p_j . Expressions (1) and (2) are the system's commodity demand and supply functions, respectively.

Functions (1) indicate that the quantities of commodities demanded, the D_j depend on the prices of these commodities, that is, on the p_j. While functions (2) indicate that the quantities of commodities supplied, the S_j also depend on the p_j.

These demand and supply functions also depend on the tastes and preferences of individuals and firms and on their resources as well as on the other variables referred to earlier. These, however, are all assumed to be fixed hence we have not shown them explicitly.

Equations (3) are the commodity excess-demand equations of Model A'. They are derived, as usual, from the commodity demand and supply functions. This is by taking the differences between the quantity demanded and supplied in each market across the system.

These differences or excess-demands, like the quantities demanded and supplied, hence also depend on the money prices, the p_j. Model A' as we pointed out is a preliminary form of the orthodox classical system, Model A.

This is because Model A' has to be adapted to ensure that it reflects rational behavior. Let us follow the literature and adapt Model A' to bring rational behavior into this system which as we shall discuss is through imposing the "homogeneity postulate" on the system.

3.4 Rational Behavior In Model A

Rational behavior requires that the demands and supplies of commodities depend only on real variables as opposed to nominal money variables. Real price variables are relative prices which are derived by taking the ratios of the money prices.

We have, however, made the demands and supplies of commodities in Model A' depend on the money prices. These money prices, however, are nominal money variables rather than real variables.

This is because a proportionate change in all money prices, which is a change in the price level, will leave the real or relative prices unchanged. This means that were behavior made to depend on the money prices, behavior would change in response to such a nominal monetary change.

This would reflect irrational behavior or what is referred to as "money illusion" since the real or relative prices have not changed.[6] Hence we shall adapt Model A' to make behavior depend only on the relative prices to ensure that behavior is rational in the system.

Model A' is characterized by n money prices of commodities. We next proceed by first obtaining the real or relative prices by taking the ratios of the n money prices. Let us denote these price ratios or relative prices which are $(n-1)$ in number, by z.

Next, we rewrite Model A' to make the quantities of commodities demanded and supplied depend only on the relative prices, that is, on the z, as opposed to the money prices. This transforms Model A' into Model A which is the system we take to represent the orthodox classical system.

Hence Model A is characterized by the "homogeneity postulate" which as we discussed earlier is the main rationale for our taking this system to be a classical system. Through this postulate we rid Model A' of "money illusion" to arrive at Model A. We show the latter system below:

Model A

4. $\quad D_j \equiv F_j[z]$

5. $\quad S_j \equiv G_j[z]$

6. $\quad E_j[z] = 0$

Behavior in Model A is rational in the sense of depending only on the real or relative prices as opposed to the money prices. This as we discussed is ensured through our imposing the "homogeneity postulate" on the system.[7]

This is reflected in Model A's demand functions, functions (4), making the quantities of commodities demanded depend only on the relative prices. As well, the system's supply functions, functions (5), also make the quantities of commodities supplied depend only on the relative prices.

These demand and supply functions then lead to Model A's excess-demand equations, equations (6). These latter

---

[6] On the orthodox concept of "money illusion" see for example, Patinkin, *op. cit.*, pps. 174-76.

[7] On the "homogeneity postulate" see also Patinkin, *op. cit.*, pps. 174-76.

equations show that the system's excess commodity demands also depend only on the relative prices. Let us now consider consistency of the system following orthodox analysis.

There are expressions implicit in Model A reflecting the demand and supply of money flows. These are derived from the money prices and the quantities of commodities demanded and supplied.

However, these expressions are dependent on the commodity equations hence they cannot be the basis for an equilibrium constraint on the system.

This means that since there are n commodities in Model A, there are n demand and n supply functions in each of (4) and (5). As a result, there are also n excess-demand equations in (6).

On the other hand, the unknowns to be determined are the relative prices which are only $(n-1)$ number. Hence the number of equations exceeds the number of unknowns which means that the system may be overdetermined and inconsistent.

That is, there are too many restrictions in the form of equations compared to variables that are imposed on the system. This means that these restrictions cannot all be met simultaneously.

There is, however, a further element to be brought into Model A which will eliminate the system's surplus equation to ensure consistency of the system. That is, to ensure that the number of independent equations equals the number of variables to be determined. This element is Say's Law which we shall now consider in detail.

3.5 Say's Law

Model A is also characterized by Say's Law which is an identity between the aggregate demand and supply of commodities.[8] Economists arrive at this identity form of the Law of the classical system in various ways.

However, most commonly, it is held that the classical economists assumed that individuals and firms sell commodities

---

[8] On Say's Law see J.B. Say, *A Treatise on Political Economy*, trans. by C.R. Prinsep (1834), pps.138-139. See also the paper by G.S Becker and W.J. Baumol, "The Classical Monetary Theory: The Outcome of the Discussion," *Economica*, XIX (1952), pps. 356-7.

only to buy other commodities. That is, commodities are exchanged only for other commodities.

This implies that the aggregate demand for commodities (ad) is identical to the aggregate supply (as) of commodities which is Say's Law. We show the Say's Law identity below:

7. $ad \equiv as$

This identity is arrived at by the quantities of commodities demanded and the quantities supplied being measured in a common unit and summed to derive the aggregate demand and supply variables in (7).

Economists then use the Say's Law identity to eliminate the surplus equation in Model A to ensure equality of the number of independent equations and unknowns in the system.

This, however, as we discussed in Chapter 1.3, is an invalid use of Say's Law which brings an incorrect form of the Law into the system. Let us review why Model A reflects an incorrect form of Say's Law then we shall review in the next section the inconsistency we uncovered in Model A.

Say's Law is a true identity in being simply a description of the overall output or income of a system alternatively as aggregate demand and aggregate supply. Hence no substantive role should be attributed to it.

Yet the Law in Model A is given the substantive role of ensuring consistency of the system. This means that the Law in Model A is an incorrect form of the Law since it is not a true identity.

This is because the Law in being a true identity should not be given the substantive role of ensuring consistency of Model A. This brings an incorrect or misused form of the Law into Model A; and it is this incorrect Say's Law that restricts the system to long-run states.

Now economists in setting out Model A do write Say's Law as an identity. However, this identity is misused in Model A in being given the substantive role described. This explains why we conclude that there is an incorrect or misused form of the Law in Model A; since a correct form of the Law should not be given the substantive role described.

Finally, we must emphasize that Say's Law in being an identity or truism cannot of itself be incorrect or inconsistent. However, we shall find it convenient to refer to Model A as being characterized by an incorrect form of the Law. This is in the sense that the Law in Model A is misused in the manner described to account for the Law in Model A not being a true identity.

3.6 Review Of The Inconsistency Of Model A

Model A is inconsistent in an economic sense because the system does not capture the general economic logic that should underlie all price systems. This is because the behavior in Model A, and hence the system's orthodox demand and supply functions, do not ensure that the system is consistent with limitation in resources.

That is, Model A's functions do not ensure that the quantities of commodities demanded (supplied) each sum to the system's limited resources to exhaust these resources.

This is a result of the system lacking the aspect to behavior described in Chapter 1.4 that should ensure that the system is consistent with limitation in resources. Model A's economic inconsistency, in turn, results in the system being initially inconsistent in that there is a surplus equation over the number of unknowns.

Economists then ensure that Model A is consistent. This is usually done by imposing Say's Law on the system to eliminate the system's surplus equation. This ensures that Model A is consistent with limitation in resources hence the system remains inconsistent   in an economic sense.

This is because Model A's economic inconsistency can only be satisfactorily resolved by revising the system's functions to make them ensure that the system is consistent with limitation in resources.

This is the course followed in this book through Model B; since Model B's functions will ensure that the system is consistent with limitation in resources. This will resolve through Model B, Model A's economic inconsistency. Moreover, we shall find that Model B automatically meets the counting rule.

This means that through Model B, we shall resolve Model A's economic inconsistency. As well, we shall resolve how this inconsistency is reflected in Model A in there being a surplus equation over the number of unknowns in the system.

Consequently, we do not need Model A's incorrect Say's Law to ensure consistency of Model B as is the case with Model A. This rids Model B of the incorrect form of the Law of Model A which restricts this system to long-run states.

In sum, Model B as will be discussed in detail later in the book is not restricted by Model A's incorrect Say's Law to long-run states. However, we shall find that Model B is yet characterized by Say's Law; but this is a correct form of the Law that is simply a descriptive device in the system that hence cannot possibly restrict the system to long-run states.

3.7 Further Remarks On How The Inconsistency Of Model A Arose And How It Will Be Resolved

Consistency in any field of study should stem from consistency of the substantive content of that field. Hence consistency of Model A should stem from the system's behavior or economic rationale. This, however, is not the case with Model A, the orthodox classical system. This system is found to be initially inconsistent.

This is because Model A does not initially meet the counting rule in that the number of independent equations and unknown variables in the system are not equal. Hence there is a gap in the behavioral rationale of Model B. This is because the behavior in the system does not ensure consistency of the system.

Next, Say's Law, which in a wholly non-behavioral element is brought into the picture to eliminate a surplus equation from Model A to ensure consistency of the system. That is, to ensure that the number of independent equations and unknowns are in the system equal.

Hence the *non-behavioral* Say's Law is made to fill the gap in the *behavioral* content of Model A. This gap, to review, exists in Model A because the behavior in the system does not ensure that the system is consistent.

Say's Law, however, in being simply an identity or truism cannot possibly fill the gap in the behavioral content of Model A. However, since the role of filling this gap is forced on the Law, this brings an incorrect form of the Law which is not a true identity into Model A; and this form of the Law restricts the system to long-run states.

Clearly, we need to bring a more general approach to the behavior of Model A that will ensure consistency of the system without having to impose Say's Law on the system. This will be accomplished through Model B, our revised classical system.

This is because we shall bring the aspect to behavior described in Chapter 1.4 into Model B. This will account for the behavior or economic rationale of this system ensuing consistency of the system. Consequently, Model B will be rid of the incorrect form of Say's Law that is imposed on Model A to ensure consistency of the system.

This will result in Model B being characterized by a correct form of Say's Law that is a true identity in being simply a descriptive device in the system. This is because Say's Law in Model B is rid of the invalid role imposed on it in Model A of ensuring consistency of the latter system.

This analysis establishes in a general way how in bringing the new aspect to behavior described in Chapter 1.4 we shall rid Model B of an incorrect form of Say's Law. This is a form of the Law that is not a true identity and which restricts Model A to long-run states. However, we can establish more precisely how this is accomplished.

Now in bringing the new aspect to behavior described in Chapter 1.4 into Model B, we shall bring a more general form of budget constraint into Model B. This is an internal budget constraint that cannot possibly restrict this system to long-run states.

This property of Model B's internal budget constraint endows it with the property of being a true identity form of Say's Law that cannot restrict the system to long-run states.

This explains more precisely how in bringing the new aspect to behavior described in Chapter 1.4, we replace the incorrect Say's Law of Model A which restricts the system to long-run states with a true identity form of the Law in Model B. This is a form of the Law that cannot possibly restrict the latter system to long-run states.

3.8 Introducing Money Into Model A

Model A, the orthodox classical system, is shown below:

Model A

4. $D_j \equiv F_j [z]$

5. $S_j \equiv G_j [z]$

6. $E_j [z] = 0$

Model A is a wholly real system since money and hence money prices or the price level are missing from it. However, we shall now proceed following orthodox analysis to bring money and hence money prices into the system.

We shall bring money and money prices into Model A by complementing the system with a long-run quantity theory of money equation. We shall use the well-known Cambridge cash-balance equation that appears below:

8. $$K\left[p_1 X_1 + p_2 X_2 + \cdots p_n X_n\right] = M$$

Let us discuss the variable K which is usually referred to as the Cambridge K. This variable represents the proportion of their money income that individuals and firms hold as a cash balance.

We also assume that these balances are held only for transactions purposes. That is, to offset any possible lack of synchronization between payments and receipts.

Next, overall money income in Model A is represented by the term $\left[p_1 X_1 + p_2 X_2 + \cdots p_n X_n\right]$ where $X_1, X_2, ..., X_n$ are the system's equilibrium quantities of commodities, each of which is multiplied by the appropriate price.

As we discussed, the variable K is the proportion of their money income that individuals and firms hold as a cash balance. Hence the whole expression to the left of the equality sign in (8) is the demand for money to hold for transactions purposes. While M to the right of (8) is the given supply of nominal money.

We next substitute the equilibrium quantities of commodities and the equilibrium relative prices from Model A into condition (8). This allows us to solve for the individual money prices or the price level from the latter condition.

As a result, we strictly followed the orthodox literature in forming Model A in two parts: first, a real part that is reflected in Model A then a monetary part that is reflected in the Cambridge equation. Then we complemented Model A with the Cambridge equation to bring money and the price level into Model A to form a monetary version of the system.

Patinkin, however, has shown that money and the price level are not satisfactorily integrated into the monetary form of Model A. This is readily confirmed.

Let us move the price level of the monetary Model A from equilibrium by making an equiproportionate change in the individual money prices. This throws the money equation (8) out of equilibrium. This should on account of Walras Law also throw the commodity markets out of equilibrium.

However, the commodity markets remain in equilibrium since as we see from the real Model A, they depend only on the relative prices which are unaffected by the change in the price level. As a result, no commodity market comes out of equilibrium to bring the price level back to equilibrium.

Consequently, the price level of the monetary Model A is indeterminate with the system as Patinkin also held being invalidly dichotomized into real and monetary parts. Walras Law, as well, is violated in the system.

Patinkin correctly held that these problems with Model A are caused by the system's "homogeneity postulate." However, we shall establish that this postulate, and hence the problems of Model A that arise from it, stem from the inconsistency in the system that has been uncovered in this book.

As a result, in resolving Model A's inconsistency through Model B, we shall rid the latter system of Model A's "homogeneity postulate" and hence of the problems of Model A we described that are caused by this postulate as will be discussed in Chapter 6.12.

This as will be discussed in Chapters 10.3 and 10.4 will account for Model A's price level indeterminacy and invalid dichotomy being resolved through Model B. More precisely, these problems will be resolved through a monetary form of Model B.

3.9 Summary

Model A, the orthodox classical price system was set out in this chapter; and we discussed how the system is initially inconsistent. Model A is then made consistent by an incorrect form of Say's Law being imposed on the system to eliminate a surplus equation.

However, while seemingly being consistent, Model A reflects the inconsistency we have uncovered in the system; and we reviewed this inconsistency and sketched how it will be resolved. We then followed the orthodox literature and added a long-run quantity theory of money equation to Model A to determine the system's price level.

Patinkin, however, has shown that Model A is dichotomized into real and monetary parts which accounts for the system's price level being indeterminate. Hence Patinkin concluded that the system is subject to an invalid dichotomy in that it causes the system's price level to be indeterminate.

However, we shall establish in Chapters 10.3 and 10.4 that these problems with Model A that Patinkin raised are resolved through Model B, our revised form of Model A. Hence Model B's price level is determinate.

Next, Model B like Model A is a dichotomized system since as in the latter system we solve for Model B's relative prices without specifying the price level. However, Model B's dichotomy does not cause the system's price level to be indeterminate. This means that Model B, unlike Model A, is characterized by a valid dichotomy.

Chapter 4

Problems With The Orthodox Classical And Neoclassical Systems

4.1 Introduction

Keynes held in the *General Theory* that Say's Law accounts for the orthodox classical system, which we represent by Model A, being restricted to describing long-run, full-employment states.

While Patinkin held that the price level of Model A, which he took as a neoclassical system, is indeterminate with the system being characterized by an invalid dichotomy between its real and monetary sectors.

We shall find that these problems with Model A that were brought out by Keynes and Patinkin arise because Model A does not reflect the general economic logic of price systems. This is on account of the inconsistency we uncover in the system.

Hence these problems with Model A can only be satisfactorily resolved by bringing the general economic logic of price systems into Model A through resolving the inconsistency in this system. This is the approach to these problems that is followed in this book through Model B.

That is, we shall resolve through Model B the inconsistency that we uncover in Model A; since this is the means whereby we isolate the general economic logic that should characterize all price systems.

This will be accomplished through our bringing the new aspect to behavior described in Chapter 1.4 into Model B. We shall thereby incorporate the general economic logic of price systems into this system. Hence through Model B, we shall generalize Model A.

This is because through Model B, we shall resolve the inconsistency of Model A that is the cause of the problems with the latter system brought out by Keynes and Patinkin. On the other hand, the Keynesian and Patinkin systems are alternatives to Model A rather than being a generalization of this system as is the case with Model B.

4.2 Keynes' Criticism Of The Classical System

Keynes in the *General Theory* imputed an identity form of Say's Law to the classical system.[9] This is a form of the Law that takes the aggregate demand for commodities to be identical to the aggregate supply; and Model A, which we use to represent the orthodox classical system, is characterized by this form of Say's Law.

This is because the Law is imposed on Model A to eliminate a surplus equation to ensure that the system is consistent. Hence Say's Law allows us to solve Model A for the system's equilibrium prices and quantities. Moreover, the Law allows for the existence of a long-run market equilibrating process that clears every market in the system.

Say's Law, to review, puts the aggregate demand for commodities identical to the aggregate supply. Hence if there are excess demands anywhere in the system, these are matched by an equal excess supply elsewhere in the system.

Economists, drawing on long-run analysis then conclude that the relative prices will instantaneously adjust to eliminate this disequilibrium in the various markets of the system without changing overall output or income.

This is a long-run, full-employment overall output or income although there will be frictional unemployment, a consequence of job search.

Keynes, however, formed a short-run or macroeconomic system where general unemployment can occur; and to do so, he had to abandon Say's Law and the perfectly flexible classical price mechanism we described that the Law implies.

Keynes then showed that there were various reasons why aggregate demand may be deficient to cause aggregate supply or overall output to fall below a full-employment level. Hence Keynes regarded his system as being more general than the classical system.

This is because the Keynesian system can describe short-run states that are characterized by general unemployment. On the other hand, the orthodox classical system is restricted by Say's Law to describing long-run, full-employment states.

What we have done is review Keynes' claim as commonly described in the literature that Model A is restricted by Say's Law

---

[9] J.M.Keynes, *The General Theory Of Employment, Interest And Money* (New York, 1936), esp. Chs. 2 and 3.

to long-run states; and we shall find that Model A is indeed restricted to long-run states by Say's Law.

However, in contrast to Keynes we establish that this is because Model A is characterized by an incorrect form of Say's Law that enters Model A system as a result of the inconsistency we uncover in the system; and it is this incorrect form of the Law that restricts Model A to long-run states.

Hence in ridding Model B of Model A's inconsistency, we shall bring a correct form of the Law into Model B; and this correct Say's Law we shall find cannot possibly restrict Model B to long-run states. Let us review why Model A reflects an incorrect form of Say's Law.

4.3 There Is An Incorrect Or Misused Form Of Say's Law In Model A

Say's Law is widely taken following Keynes to account for the orthodox classical system, which we represent by Model A, being restricted to describing long-run full-employment states. However, we shall find that this is due to the economic inconsistency that we uncover in the system.

This inconsistency arises because Model A's functions do not ensure that the system is consistent with limitation in resources. That is, Model A's functions do not ensure that the quantities of commodities demanded (supplied) each sum to the system's limited resources to exhaust these resources.

This is because the aspect to behavior described in Chapter 1.4 that should ensure that the system is consistent with limitation in resources is missing from the system. This results in Model A being initially inconsistent.

Say's Law is then imposed on the system to eliminate a surplus equation to ensure consistency of the system; and this as we have established, ensures that Model A is consistent with limitation in resources.

This means, however, that Say's Law is used in the attempt to make Model A, which is inconsistent in an economic sense. This misuse of Say's Law in Model A then results in an incorrect form of the Law entering the system.

This incorrect Say's Law is not a true identity and it restricts Model A to long-run states. We note that economists in setting out Model A do write Say's Law as an identity.

However, this identity is misused in Model A in being given the substantive role in Model A of eliminating a surplus equation to ensure consistency of the system. This explains why we conclude that there is an incorrect form or misused of the Law in Model A; since a correct form of the Law should not be given the substantive role we described.

Now in resolving Model A's economic inconsistency through Model B we shall find as will be discussed in Chapter 6.4, that the latter system is automatically consistent in the sense that it automatically meets the counting rule. Hence we do not need Say's Law to make Model B consistent.

This rids Model B of Model A's incorrect form of Say's Law which is not a true identity; and this results in Model B being characterized by a correct form of the Law. This is a form of the Law that is a true identity hence it cannot have any substantive influence in Model B.

This is because as we established in Chapter 2.7, it is solely a descriptive device in the system, a finding we shall confirm in Chapter 6.3. As a result, Model B's Say's Law cannot possibly account for the system being restricted to long-run states.

Instead, Model B will describe long-run states on account of the behavior in the system rather than on account of Say's Law. This is because we shall establish in Chapter 7.3 that Model B is consistent with the existence of behavioral long-run market processes.

4.4 How The Restriction Of Model A To Long-Run States Will Be Resolved

We discussed in Section 4.2 of the chapter how Keynes held that Model A is restricted to long-run states by Say's Law. True, Model A is restricted to long-run states by Say's Law; but this is because the Law to which Keynes referred is an incorrect or misused form of the Law.

Were it a correct form of the Law it could not possibly restrict Model A to long-run states. This is because a correct form of the Law is a true identity that is simply a descriptive device in a system hence it can have no substantive influence in a system.

We are now in a position to sketch how through Model B we shall resolve the problem of Model A being restricted to long-run states.

Economists clearly recognize that Say's Law is a true identity in that they create it by describing the overall output or income of a system alternatively as aggregate demand and aggregate supply. Hence the Law is simply a descriptive device in a system which explains why it is a true identity.

Economists, however, do not ensure that the Law is indeed a true identity when they write Model A. This is because the Law in Model A is given the substantive role of eliminating a surplus equation from the system to ensure consistency of the system.

Hence the form of the Law that actually characterizes Model A, in having such a substantive role, is not a true identity which means that it is not a correct form of the Law; and it is this incorrect form of the Law that restricts Model A to long-run states.

However, Model A's incorrect Say's Law provides the basis for a budget constraint of relevance to microeconomics in that individual quantities of commodities emerge from this budget constraint. This accounts for Model A being wholly microeconomic in character.

Now we shall bring a true identity form of Say's Law into Model B. Hence we shall resolve through Model B the problem of Model A being restricted to long-run states by an incorrect form of Say's Law.

Moreover, as discussed in Chapter 2.8, we shall find that on account of Model B's true identity form of Say's Law, we correctly bring into this system a budget constraint of relevance to microeconomics. This accounts for Model B being wholly microeconomic in character.

Consequently, Model B unlike Model A will not be restricted to long-run states by an incorrect form of Say's Law. Keynes also rid his system of Model A's incorrect or misused form of the Law but this was through Keynes allowing the aggregate demand and supply of commodities in his system to diverge.

However, as we discussed in Chapter 2.8, Keynes' approach to ridding his system of Model A's incorrect form of Say's Law suppresses the microeconomics of the real part of his system. This issue will be covered in fuller detail in Chapter 9.

4.5 Patinkin's Criticisms Of The Neoclassical System

Model A which Patinkin took as a neoclassical system is characterized by the "homogeneity postulate." Patinkin then showed that this postulate invalidly dichotomizes the system into real and monetary parts.

As well, Patinkin showed that this postulate accounts for Model A's price level being indeterminate with Walras Law also being violated in the system. Patinkin hence concluded that the system is inconsistent.

However, it was later shown by Hickman, Valavanis and a number of other economists that Model A may be looked on as being a formally consistent system. This is in the sense that it can be solved for equilibrium; and Patinkin agreed that Model A may be considered in this sense to be consistent.[10]

Patinkin, however, held that this issue of the formal consistency of Model A was not in question and was not relevant to what he held was the main problem with Model A. This is that the system is inconsistent in an economic sense.

This inconsistency results in Model A being unable to describe behavior out of equilibrium. Hence the system cannot deal with basic monetary issues such as the stability of monetary equilibrium.

Next, Patinkin formed his real-balance system where real balances are introduced as a determinant of behavior. Moreover, Patinkin held that through his real-balance system he resolved the issues of the price level indeterminacy and invalid dichotomy of Model A.

We shall find, however, that Patinkin's criticism that Model A is inconsistent in an economic sense, in being characterized by these problems, is of relevance to this book.

This is because we shall find that Model B through which we resolve the inconsistency of Model A, is consistent with the existence of market equilibrating processes. This means as we shall discuss in Chapter 10.3 and Chapter 10.4, that through Model B we resolve the price level indeterminacy and related problems of Model A brought out by Patinkin,

Hence Model A is indeed inconsistent in an economic sense as Patinkin claimed in being characterized by the problems we described that Patinkin brought out. However, Model A's economic inconsistency arises because of the inconsistency in the system that we uncover in this book.

This means that Patinkin, although taking Model A to be inconsistent in an economic sense, did not uncover the economic inconsistency in the system that we have uncovered in this book.

Consequently, Patinkin in not uncovering this inconsistency did not uncover the underlying cause of Model A's

---

[10] On these issues see Patinkin, *op.cit.*, Ch.VIII and pps. 624-29.

inconsistency that results in the price level indeterminacy and related problems of the system.

However, through resolving Model A's inconsistency through Model B, we shall as will be discussed in Chapter 10, rid the latter system of the problems of Model A brought out by Patinkin. Hence Model B will be a generalization of Model A.

On the other hand Patinkin in his real balance system bypassed the inconsistency of Model A. As a result, he left Model A untouched and hence still characterized by the problems with the system that he uncovered.

True, the price level of Patinkin's real balance system is determinate. However, as Patinkin recognized the real balance effect that accounts for the determinacy of the price level of his system does not operate in the long-run Model A.

This confirms that Patinkin left Model A untouched and hence still characterized by the problems he had uncovered. Consequently, Patinkin's real balance system is an alternative to Model A.

On the other hand, through Model B we shall as will be discussed in Chapter 10, resolve the problems with Model A brought out by Patinkin. Hence Model B is a generalization of Model A rather than being an alternative to the latter system.

4.6 Resolving The Problems With Model A Brought Up By Keynes And Patinkin

We have discussed how Keynes held that Model A is restricted to long-run states by Say's Law. While Patinkin showed that the price level of Model A is indeterminate with the system also being subject to an invalid real-monetary dichotomy.

These problems with Model A are *symptoms or consequences* of the underlying inconsistency that we uncover in the system. Hence these problems can only be satisfactorily resolved through resolving this inconsistency of Model A. This will be accomplished through Model B.

As a result, we shall rid Model B of the problems of Model A brought out by Keynes and Patinkin. This means that Model B is a generalization of Model A. On the other hand, the Keynesian and Patinkin systems bypass the inconsistency of Model B hence these systems are alternatives to Model A.

Let us discuss in more detail why Model B is a generalization of Model A whereas the Keynesian and Patinkin systems are alternatives to Model A.

Keynes held that Model A is restricted to long-run states by Say's Law. However, we show that this is because the Law in Model A is an incorrect form of the Law; and it is this incorrect Law that restricts the system to long-run states.

Hence to resolve this problem with Model A, we need to bring a correct form of the Law into the system. This is the course we follow in this book through Model B. This reflects how Model B is a generalization of Model A.

Keynes, in contrast, wholly rid his system of Model A's incorrect Say's Law while leaving Model A untouched and hence still characterized by an incorrect form of the Law. This reflects how the Keynesian system is an alternative to Model A. Let us next consider the Patinkin system.

Patinkin correctly held that Model A's "homogeneity postulate" accounts for the system being characterized by an indeterminate price level and invalid real-monetary dichotomy. He then wholly rid his system of Model A's "homogeneity postulate" while leaving Model A untouched. This reflects how the Patinkin system is an alternative to Model A.

In sum, Keynes and Patinkin formed systems that are alternatives to Model A. This is reflected in Keynes and Patinkin both leaving Model A untouched and hence still characterized by the problems with the system they had uncovered.

On the other hand, Model B is a generalization of Model A. Let us discuss what accounts for this difference between Model B on the one hand and the Keynesian and Patinkin systems on the other.

4.7 Remarks On The New Approach To Price Systems

Model B is based on an approach that focuses on the general economic logic that should underlie all price systems rather than on the specific forms of behavior of individual systems. This is through our focusing on how consistency with limitation in resources is ensured in the systems.

Next, all price systems should reflect behavior that is consistent with limitation in resources. Hence in focusing on consistency of the systems with limitation in resources, we focus on the general logic of the systems.

Our pursuing this issue of how consistency of price systems with limitation in resource is to be ensured led us to uncover and resolve, through Model B, the inconsistency in the orthodox classical system, Model A.

This allows us to arrive through Model B at a very general approach to price systems. This is because in dealing with consistency of price systems with limitation in resources, we deal with the general logic that should characterize all price systems.

Moreover, we arrive through Model B at a correct approach to ensuring consistency of price systems with limitation in resources. This is reflected in Model B being made consistent with limitation in resources by the behavior in the system. This means that Model B reflects the general *economic* logic of price systems.

On the other hand, we established that Model A is made consistent with limitation in resources as a result of Say's Law being imposed on the system to eliminate a surplus equation.

Hence while Model A reflects the general logic of price systems in reflecting consistency with limitation in resources, Model A does not reflect the general *economic* logic of price systems. This brought inconsistency into Model A, an inconsistency resolved through Model B; since this system reflects the general economic logic of price systems.

Now the Keynesian and Patinkin systems do not deal with the general economic logic that should characterize all price systems but with the specific forms of behavior of these individual systems.

Hence the Keynesian and Patinkin systems cannot possibly resolve the inconsistency of Model A. This is because this is an inconsistency that is due to the general economic logic of price systems being suppressed in Model A.

This explains why the Keynesian and Patinkin systems are alternatives to Model A. This also explains why the Keynesian and Patinkin systems cannot resolve in a satisfactory manner the problems with Model A brought up by Keynes and Patinkin.

This is because to satisfactorily resolve these problems with Model A requires that we resolve the underlying inconsistency of the system that stems from the system's general logic being non-behavioral rather than behavioral or economic in character.

This is accomplished through Model B; since through this system, we resolve the inconsistency of Model A through bringing the general *economic* logic of price systems into Model B. This is through our bringing the new aspect to behavior described in Chapter 1.4 that is missing from Model A into Model B.

This explains why Model B is a generalization of Model A rather than being an alternative to Model A as is the case with the Keynesian and Patinkin systems. Hence these latter two systems, in being alternatives to Model A, could not possibly get to the root cause of the problems with Model A which is the inconsistency that we uncover in the system.

We may also bring out in the following way why the Keynesian and Patinkin systems are alternatives to Model A whereas Model B is a generalization of Model A.

Keynes showed that Model A is restricted to long-run states by Say's Law. While Patinkin showed that Model A is subject to an invalid real-monetary and price level indeterminacy. Keynes and Patinkin then approached these problems of Model A through their systems.

However, these problems of Model A that were brought out by Keynes and Patinkin are *symptoms or consequences* of the underlying inconsistency in Model A uncovered in this book.

Hence Keynes and Patinkin in approaching these problems of Model A through their systems, dealt with these symptoms or consequences of the underlying inconsistency of Model A uncovered in this book rather than with this inconsistency itself.

However, to satisfactorily resolve the problems with Model A that were brought out by Keynes and Patinkin, we need to resolve the underlying inconsistency in the system uncovered in this book that is the cause of these problems.

This is the approach to these problems followed in this book through Model B; since through this system, we resolve the underlying inconsistency in Model A that is the cause of these problems. Clearly, this accounts for Model B being a generalization of Model A.

Keynes and Patinkin, however, bypass in their systems the underlying inconsistency in Model A that is the cause of the problems with this system that they uncovered. This explains why the Keynesian and Patinkin systems are alternatives to Model A whereas Model B is a generalization of Model A.

4.8 Summary

Keynes held in the *General Theory* that Say's Law accounts for the orthodox classical system, which we represent by Model A, being restricted to describing long-run, full-employment states.

While Patinkin held that the price level of Model A, which he took as a neoclassical system, is indeterminate with the system being characterized by an invalid dichotomy between its real and monetary sectors.

67

We shall find that these problems with Model A that were brought out by Keynes and Patinkin arise because Model A does not reflect the general economic logic of price systems. This is on account of the inconsistency that we uncover in the system.

Hence these problems can only be satisfactorily resolved by bringing the general economic logic of price systems into Model A through resolving the inconsistency in this system. This is the approach to these problems that is followed in this book through Model B, our revised form of Model A.

That is, we resolve through Model B the inconsistency that we uncover in Model A; since this is the means whereby we isolate the general economic logic that should characterize all price systems.

This is accomplished by our bringing the new aspect to behavior described in Chapter 1.4 into Model B. We shall thereby incorporate this general economic logic into this system. This means that through Model B, we generalize Model A.

This is because through Model B, we resolve the inconsistency of Model A that is the cause of the problems with the latter system brought out by Keynes and Patinkin. Model B hence becomes a generalization of Model A.

In contrast, Keynes and Patinkin in their systems bypass the inconsistency of Model A that is due to the aspect to behavior described in Chapter 1.4 being missing from the latter system. As a result, Keynes and Patinkin left Model A untouched and hence still characterized by the problems with the system that they uncovered.

Consequently, Keynes and Patinkin formed systems that are alternatives to Model A. Whereas through Model B, we revise and generalize Model A since Model B will be rid of the problems with Model A that were brought out by Keynes and Patinkin.

We also brought out in the chapter in the following way why the Keynesian and Patinkin systems are alternatives to Model A whereas Model B is a generalization of Model A.

To review, Keynes showed that Model A is restricted to long-run states by Say's Law. While Patinkin showed that Model A is subject to an invalid real-monetary dichotomy and price level indeterminacy. Keynes and Patinkin then approached these problems of Model A through their systems.

These problems, however, are *symptoms or consequences* of the underlying inconsistency in Model A uncovered in this book. Hence Keynes and Patinkin in approaching these problems of Model A through their systems, dealt with these symptoms or consequences of the inconsistency of Model A uncovered in this book rather than with this inconsistency itself.

In contrast, through Model B we resolve the underlying inconsistency in Model A that is the cause of these problems with the latter system that were brought out by Keynes and Patinkin. These issues as they concern the Keynesian system will be covered in more detail in Chapter 8.6.

Chapter 5

The Rationale Of The New Approach To Price Systems

5.1 Introduction

We uncover in this book an inconsistency in the orthodox classical price system, Model A. This inconsistency arises because an aspect to the behavior of individuals and firms is missing from the system. This is the aspect to behavior that should ensure that the system is consistent with limitation in resources.

More precisely, this is the aspect to behavior that should ensure that the quantities of commodities demanded and supplied each sum to Model A's limited resources to hence exhaust these resources.

Next, all price systems must reflect behavior that is consistent with limitation in resources. Hence since the aspect to behavior described is missing from Model A consistency of the system with limitation in resource is ensured as a result of the non-behavioral Say's Law being imposed on the system.

This brings inconsistency into Model A; since consistency of the system with limitation in resource should be ensured by the behavior in the system.

This means as we discussed earlier that Model A does not reflect the general *economic* logic of price systems. Model A does indeed reflect the *general logic* of price systems in reflecting consistency with limitation in resources.

However, Model A does not reflect the general economic logic of price systems; since consistency of the system with limitation in resources is not ensured by the behavior in the system.

We described the aspect to behavior that is missing from Model A in Chapter 1.4. As well, we sketched in Chapters 1.6 and 1.7 the implications of this new aspect to behavior for the budget constraints of Model A and Model B. However, we shall cover these analyses in more detail in this chapter.

Then in the next chapter, we shall formally set out Model B into which we shall integrate this new aspect to behavior. This will account for us resolving through Model B, the economic inconsistency we have uncovered in Model A.

5.2 Limitation In Resources And The Budget Constraints Of Price Systems

We discussed in Chapter 1.3 how there is an economic inconsistency in Model A, the orthodox classical system. This inconsistency arises because Model A's functions do not capture the general economic logic that should underlie all price systems.

This is because consistency of Model A with limitation in resources is not ensured by the system's functions and hence is not ensured by the behavior in the system.

Instead, Model A is made consistent with limitation in resources as a result of the system's incorrect form of Say's Law being imposed on the system to eliminate a surplus equation.

This brings inconsistency into Model A; since the system should be made consistent with limitation in resources by the behavior in the system rather than by the non-behavioral Say's Law.

Next, budget constraints arise in price systems as a result of limitation in resources in the systems. Hence we would expect that Model A, in not dealing satisfactorily with limitation in resources, is characterized by an incorrect budget constraint. This, we shall find, is the case.

This is because we shall find that Model A is subject to a budget constraint that is imposed on the system from outside the system by an incorrect or misused form of Say's Law; and this external budget constraint restricts the system to long-run states.

However, in resolving Model A's inconsistency through Model B, we shall deal satisfactorily with limitation in resources in the latter system. Hence we would expect that Model B has a satisfactory budget constraint; and this is also the case.

This is because we shall find that Model B is characterized by a budget constraint that is determined internally in the system. Hence this budget constraint cannot possibly restrict the system to long-run states.

On the other hand, we shall find that Model A is characterized by an external budget constraint that restricts this system to long-run states.

This will explain why Model A is characterized by an incorrect form of Say's Law while Model B, in being characterized by an internal budget constraint, reflects a correct form of the Law.

This is because Say's Law in Model B is solely a descriptive device in the system as was established in Chapter 2.7, a finding that will be confirmed in Chapter 6.3. Let us put this analysis in the following way. We deal with Say's Law in Model A and Model B by dealing with the Law in these systems in terms of budget constraints.

Then we show that the Law in Model A is an external budget constraint that restricts the system to long-run states. This allows us to establish that the Law in Model A is an incorrect form of the Law that is not a true identity.

Next, we show that the Law in Model B is an internal budget constraint that cannot possibly restrict the system to long-run states. This allows us to establish that the Law in Model B is a correct form of the Law that is a true identity.

5.3 The Limited Resources Of Price Systems

Model A, the orthodox form of the classical system, appears below:

Model A

4. $\quad D_j \equiv F_j\,[z]$

5. $\quad S_j \equiv G_j\,[z]$

6. $\quad E_j\,[z] \vdash 0$

Next, the Say's Law identity that was set out in Chapter 3.5 is imposed on the system to eliminate a surplus equation to make the system consistent.

This identity which is shown below puts the aggregate demand for commodities (ad) identical to the aggregate supply (as) of commodities. This identity is then imposed on Model A to eliminate a surplus equation to make the system consistent:

7. $\quad ad \equiv as$

We derive the aggregate demand (ad) and aggregate supply (as) variables in expression (7) by measuring the individual quantities of commodities demanded (supplied) in a common unit. Then we sum these quantities to derive the aggregate demand and supply variables in expression (7).

Model A's incorrect Say's Law, to review, is imposed on the system to eliminate a surplus equation to make the system consistent. Hence we can solve the system for its equilibrium quantities and equilibrium prices.

Next, Model A like all price systems is necessarily subject to limitation in resources. Consequently, there should be a variable in the system that we may take as reflecting the system's limited resources. We isolated this variable which we denoted by W in Chapter 1.6.

This variable reflects the overall output or income of both Model A and Model B as well as the systems' limited flow of resources. However, Model B will have a more general character than Model A. This is because we shall bring the new aspect to behavior described in Chapter 1.4 into Model B.

This behavior first takes individuals and firms in Model B as being aware that their resources, as reflected in the variable W, are limited. This brings W into the behavioral content of Model B. That is, into the system's demand and supply functions.

This is how we shall capture in Model B that individuals and firms in this system are aware that their resources are limited which is the first facet to the behavior described in Chapter 1.4. Then Model B will capture the second facet to this behavior.

This is through individuals and firms determining relative quantities of commodities demanded (supplied). Hence the quantities demanded (supplied) in being relative quantities demanded (supplied) each adjust in a relative manner to always sum to the variable W. Consequently, Model B will reflect the overall aspect to behavior described in Chapter 1.4.

This behavior, in turn, will account for Model B being made consistent with limitation in resources. Hence through Model B we shall, as will now be discussed, resolve the inconsistency we uncovered in Model A.

Now the variable W of Model A although being identical to that of Model B, remains outside the behavioral content of Model A; since W is imposed on Model A by the system's incorrect or misused form of Say's Law.

Hence the W of Model A in being outside the system's behavioral content cannot possibly reflect how individuals and firms are aware that their resources are limited.

This suppresses in Model A what is a key postulate of this book which is that individuals and firms are aware that their resources are limited.

This as will be discussed in Chapter 6.8 causes the other facet to the behavior described in Chapter 1.4 to be suppressed in Model A. Hence the overall behavior described in Chapter 1.4 that characterizes Model B is suppressed in Model A which brings inconsistency into the system.

5.4 The Budget Constraints Of Model A And Model B

Model B, our revised classical system, reflects a new aspect to the behavior of individuals and firms, an aspect to behavior that was described in Chapter 1.4. This aspect to behavior first implies that individuals and firms are aware that their resources are limited.

Next, as we discussed in Chapter 1.6, Model A is characterized by the variable W which reflects the system's limited flow of resources. However, W is imposed on Model A by the system's incorrect Say's Law. This means that W remains outside the system's behavioral content.

Hence the new aspect to behavior described in Chapter 1.4 that we bring into Model B, is suppressed in Model A. This is because W in being outside Model A's behavioral content cannot possibly reflect how individuals and firms are aware that their resources are limited.

In contrast, Model B reflects this new aspect to behavior. This means that individuals and firms in Model B are aware that their resources are limited.

This moves W from outside the behavioral content of Model A, where it was put by the system's incorrect Say's Law, into the behavioral content of Model B. This is how individuals and firms in the latter system are made aware that their resources are limited.

Now the new aspect to behavior in Model B also implies that individuals and firms act in light of their awareness that their resources are limited. This is reflected in individuals and firms determining relative quantities of commodities demanded (supplied).

As a result, the quantities of commodities demanded (supplied) in Model B, in being relative quantities demanded (supplied), each adjust in a relative manner to always sum to W. That is, to always exhaust Model B's limited flow resources.

This gives rise to a budget constraint in Model B that is determined within the system. This means that this budget constraint cannot possibly restrict Model B to long-run states. This is because it is not imposed on the system from the outside but is determined within the system.

Next, individual quantities of commodities demanded (supplied) emerge from Model B's internal budget constraint. This accounts for Model B being wholly microeconomic in character. Now Model A is characterized by the identical variable W that exists in Model B. However, Model A lacks the new aspect to behavior that we brought into Model B.

Hence the variable W is not taken by individuals and firms in Model A to reflect their limited flow of resources. This results in W remaining outside the latter system's behavioral content where it was put by the system's incorrect Say's Law.

Nonetheless, as in Model B, the variable W also reflects the limited flow of resources of Model A. Hence W also provides the basis for a budget constraint in Model A. Model A's budget constraint, however, is an external budget constraint.

This is because the variable W that gives rise to this budget constraint is outside the system's behavioral content; and this external budget constraint restricts Model A to long-run states.

However, Model A's external budget constraint provides the basis for the system to be wholly microeconomic in character. This is because individual quantities of commodities demanded (supplied) emerge from Model A's external budget constraint which accounts for the system being wholly microeconomic in character.

In sum, both Model A and Model B are wholly microeconomic in character. However, Model A is restricted to long-run states by an external budget constraint form of Say's Law. Model B, however, is characterized by an internal budget form of Say's Law that cannot possibly restrict this system to long-run states.

5.5 Replacing Model A's Demand And Supply Functions With Model B's Functions

We discussed in Chapter 1.6 how we isolated the variable W that reflects the limited flow of resources of both Model A and Model B. Next, the new aspect to behavior that characterizes Model B brings W from outside the behavioral content of Model A into the behavioral content of Model B.

This is because the first facet to this new aspect to behavior of Model B results in individuals and firms taking W as reflecting their limited flow of resources. This accounts for W being brought from outside the behavioral content of Model A, where it was put by the system's incorrect Say's Law, into the behavioral content of Model B.

This means that it is the new aspect to behavior of Model B that rids this system of Model A's external budget constraint form of Say's Law; since on account of this new aspect to behavior, Model A's external budget constraint disappears from the system and re-appears as an internal budget constraint in Model B.

Next, we must ensure that the quantities of commodities demanded and supplied in Model B each sum to W to cause these quantities to emerge from the system's internal budget constraint.

Clearly, we could not draw on Model A's functions to ensure this; since this would bring Model A's external budget constraint form of Say's Law back into the system. This explains why in Model B we shift from Model A's functions to Model B's relative demand and supply functions.

Now Model B's internal functions that were described in Chapter 2.4 are within the system's overall demand and supply functions. That is, they exist within the system's behavioral content.

As a result, these functions, in being internal to Model B, can operate on the W of Model B. This is because this W as we discussed is now also within Model B's behavioral content.

This accounts for these internal functions of Model B operating on W to determine quantities of commodities demanded and supplied that always sum to W. This reflects how Model A's external budget constraint is re-created within Model B as an internal budget constraint.

Moreover, Model B's internal budget constraint reflects a true identity form of Say's Law that cannot possibly restrict this system to long-run states.

This is because as we discussed in Chapter 2.7 and will confirm in Chapter 6.3, the Law is simply a descriptive device in Model B which explains why it cannot possibly restrict the latter system to long-run states.

5.6 How Model A Is Made Consistent With Limitation In Resources

We show Model A the orthodox classical system below:

Model A

4. $\quad D_j \equiv F_j\,[z]$

5. $\quad S_j \equiv G_j\,[z]$

6. $\quad E_j\,[z] = 0$

Next, the Say's Law identity is also shown again below:

7. $\qquad ad \equiv as$

Model A is initially inconsistent in that there is a surplus equation over the number of unknowns. Say's Law is then imposed on the system to eliminate this surplus equation to ensure consistency of the system.

Let us now refer to the variable W which was first introduced in Chapter 1.6 and which reflects Model A's limited flow of resources.

In imposing Model A's incorrect Say's Law on the system to make it consistent, we impose the variable W on the system. Consequently, W remains outside the system's behavioral content.

Next, since W reflects Model A's limited flow of resources, the n quantities demanded and the n quantities supplied in the system must each sum to W.

Model A's demand and supply functions, however, initially determine absolute quantities of commodities demanded and supplied. Hence these quantities will not necessarily sum to the variable W.

These quantities, however, will each always sum to W if they are transformed into *relative* quantities demanded and *relative* quantities supplied.

This is because in being transformed into relative quantities demanded (supplied), the quantities demanded (supplied) in Model A will each adjust in a relative manner to always sum to the variable W.

Hence in imposing Say's Law on Model A to make the system consistent, we transform the quantities of commodities demanded (supplied) in the system into relative quantities demanded (supplied). This ensures that Model A is consistent with limitation in resources.

This, to review, is because these quantities demanded (supplied) in Model A, in being transformed into relative quantities demanded (supplied), will each adjust in a relative manner to always sum to W that reflects the system's limited flow of resources.

Consequently, Model A has a relative character or relative element. However, Model A's relative character or element is not made explicit and brought into the system through the system's demand and supply functions.

That is, the process we described whereby the quantities in Model A are transformed into relative quantities does not have a behavioral foundation. This is because it is a result of Say's Law being imposed on the system to make it consistent.

We are now, however, in a position to discuss how we shall revise and generalize Model A, through Model B, to give this process that we isolated in Model A, a behavioral foundation in Model B. This will account for Model B having a more general character than Model A.

5.7 Revising And Generalizing Model A Through Model B

We discussed in the preceding section of the chapter how Model A has a relative character or relative element. However, this relative character or relative element is not made explicit and brought into the system through the system's demand and supply functions.

That is, this relative character or element of Model A does not stem from the behavior in the system hence it does not have a behavioral foundation. However, we shall revise and generalize Model A, through Model B, by making the relative element of Model A that is implicit in this system, explicit in Model B.

Then we shall bring this relative element into Model B through the system's demand and supply functions. That is, we shall explicitly take the quantities of commodities demanded (supplied) in Model B to be relative quantities demanded (supplied).

We shall then write Model B's demand and supply functions to determine relative quantities of commodities demanded (supplied); and we shall make these relative quantities demanded (supplied) depend only on the relative prices. That is,

Model B's relative character, unlike that of Model A, will be given a behavioral foundation.

As a result, Model B's demand and supply functions will ensure that the system is consistent with limitation in resources; since the quantities demanded (supplied), in being relative quantities, will each adjust in a relative manner to always sum to W, the system's limited flow of resources.

Hence consistency of Model B with limitation in resources will be ensured by the system's behavior or economic rationale in being ensured by the system's demand and supply functions. This means that through Model B, we shall resolve Model A's economic inconsistency.

This, to review, is because Model A's economic inconsistency arises because consistency of the system with limited resources is ensured as a result of Say's Law being imposed on the system to eliminate a surplus equation from the system. This transforms the quantities in the system into relative quantities.

However, we shall give this role of Say's Law in Model A of determining relative quantities to the behavior of Model B. That is, to the latter system's demand and supply functions. This will account for Model B, unlike Model A, capturing the general economic logic that should underlie all price systems.

This in turn, will account for us resolving through Model B, the inconsistency that we have uncovered in Model A; since Model A's inconsistency arises because the general economic logic of price systems is suppressed in this system.

5.8 The Rationale Of Model B's Demand And Supply Functions

An economic inconsistency enters Model A because consistency of the system with limitation in resources is not ensured by the system's behavior or economic rationale.

That is, Model A's functions do not ensure that the quantities determined in the system sum to the system's limited resources.

Instead, consistency of the system with limitation in resources is ensured as a result of the system being made consistent by an incorrect form of Say's Law being imposed on the system to eliminate a surplus equation.

Next, we showed in Section 5.6 that this is through the quantities of commodities in Model A being transformed into relative quantities by Say's Law being imposed on the system. This provides us with a clue as to how Model A's hidden inconsistency may be resolved.

Say's Law to review, ensures consistency of Model A with limited resources by transforming the quantities in the system into relative quantities. This raises the possibility that there may be a way to avoid having to use Say's Law to ensure that Model A is consistent with limitation in resources.

That is some way other than through Say's Law to transform the quantities in the system into relative quantities. This will be accomplished by our making Model B's demand and supply functions determine relative quantities of commodities demanded and relative quantities supplied.

This leads to the new type of demand and supply functions of Model B to be set out in this book, functions to be called *relative demand and supply functions*.

This is because these functions, to be set out formally in the next chapter, will determine *relative* quantities of commodities demanded and *relative* quantities of commodities supplied.

Moreover, these relative quantities of commodities demanded and relative quantities supplied will be made to depend only on the relative prices to give rise to our new type of demand and supply functions. These new demand and supply functions will become the basis for Model B, our revised form of Model A.

Then through Model B, we shall resolve the economic inconsistency of Model A. This is because Model B's functions, and hence the behavior in the system, will ensure that the system is consistent with limitation in resources.

This is because Model B's functions will determine relative quantities of commodities demanded (supplied). Hence these quantities, in being relative quantities, will adjust in a relative manner to always exhaust the system's limited resources.

Finally, the generality of Model B is due to the system's demand and supply functions reflecting the new aspect to behavior described in Chapter 1.4. On the other hand, this aspect to behavior is missing from Model A's functions.

Consequently, this new aspect to behavior of Model B requires that we shift from Model A's orthodox or neoclassical-type demand and supply to Model B's new type of demand and supply functions. This is because the latter functions will reflect the new aspect to behavior that we bring into Model B. These issues will be covered in detail in Chapter 6.6.

5.9 Summary

We uncover in this book an economic inconsistency in the orthodox classical system, Model A. This inconsistency arises because an aspect to the behavior of individuals and firms is missing from the system.

This is the aspect to behavior that is required to ensure that the system is consistent with limitation in resources. However, we shall bring this aspect to behavior into Model B which means that through this system we shall resolve Model A's economic inconsistency.

This inconsistency led to Model A being characterized by an external budget constraint that restricts the system to long-run states. This external budget constraint, however, will be replaced in Model B by an internal budget constraint that cannot possibly restrict this latter system to long-run states.

This chapter also brought out how we approach price systems by explicitly taking the systems as being necessarily *subject* to limitation in resources. This led us to focus on how *consistency* of the systems with limitation in resources is to be ensured.

Carrying out this analysis required isolating a variable in the systems that we may take to reflect the systems' limited resources; and we isolated such a variable in Chapter 1.6.

This variable, which we denoted by W, reflects the limited *flow* of resources of both Model A and Model B; and it brings up the issue of how consistency with limitation in resources is ensured in these systems.

Then in focusing on how consistency of Model A with the system's limited resources is ensured, we uncovered the inconsistency we have described that characterizes this system.

Moreover, focusing on how consistency with these limited resources is ensured in Model B allowed us to uncover, and ultimately resolve, Model A's inconsistency through Model B.

We also discussed how the generality of Model B is due to the system's demand and supply functions reflecting the new aspect to behavior described in Chapter 1.4. On the other hand, this aspect to behavior is missing from Model A's functions.

This means that this new aspect to behavior of Model B requires that we shift from Model A's orthodox or neoclassical-type demand and supply to Model B's new type of demand and supply functions. This will be discussed in detail in Chapter 6.6.

Chapter 6

Revision Of The Orthodox Classical System

6.1 Introduction

We described earlier the inconsistency in Model A, the orthodox classical price system and the problems caused by this inconsistency. As well, we discussed in the preceding chapter how this inconsistency will be resolved.

This is through our revising the orthodox or neoclassical-type demand and supply functions of Model A, through Model B's demand and supply functions, along the lines discussed in Chapter 5.8.

Revision of Model A's functions will be carried out in this chapter which leads to our relative demand and supply functions. These new functions will provide the basis for Model B, our revised classical system, which is set out formally in this chapter; and through this system, we shall resolve the inconsistency that we have uncovered in Model A.

Next, the basis of Model B lies in the new aspect to behavior that we shall bring into the system through our new type of demand and supply functions; and we shall discuss in detail in Sections 6.8 and 6.9 of the chapter how this new aspect to behavior is brought into Model B as well as how it is suppressed in Model A.

6.2 Properties Of The Revised Classical System

Model B our revised classical system, like Model A, is also a long-run system. However, the systems differ significantly. This is because we approach our new systems, which we represent by Model B, by pursuing the issue of how consistency of price systems with limitation in resources is to be ensured.

That is, by pursuing the issue of how consistency of the general logic of price systems is to be ensured. This approach is based on our bringing into our new systems, the aspect to the behavior of individuals and firms that we described in Chapter 1.4, an aspect to behavior that is missing from Model A.

This aspect to behavior, in turn, leads to a new way of looking at the quantities of commodities in price systems. This is that these quantities must be taken to be behaviorally-determined relative quantities.

We shall capture this through our new type of demand and supply functions of Model B; since these functions will determine relative quantities of commodities demanded and relative quantities supplied as functions of the relative prices.

Hence these quantities, in being relative quantities, will adjust in a relative manner to always sum to Model B's limited resources. As a result, our relative demand and supply functions of Model B will ensure that the system is consistent with limitation in resources.

This means that the behavior in the system will ensure consistency of the system with limitation in resources. That is, Model B will reflect the general *economic* logic that should characterize all price systems. Hence through Model B we shall resolve the economic inconsistency of Model A.

This, to review, is because Model A's economic inconsistency arises because the system is made consistent with limitation in resources as a result Say's Law being imposed on the system to eliminate a surplus equation. Hence Model A, unlike Model B, does not reflect the general *economic* logic that should underlie all price systems. This brings inconsistency into Model A

6.3 The Revised Classical System

Model B's functions will make *relative* quantities of commodities demanded, and *relative* quantities of commodities supplied, depend on the relative prices. These functions also depend on other variables which are fixed and hence will not be shown explicitly. These are the same variables as those of Model A.

These are the tastes and preferences of individuals and firms as well as their resources. Moreover, population and the state of technology are held fixed. As in Model A, there are n quantities of commodities in our revised classical system, Model B.

As well, we shall continue to denote the quantities of commodities demanded by D_j and the quantities supplied by S_j, where $j=1,2,3,...,n$; and we also use the variable z to denote the relative prices of Model B as was done in the case of

Model A. These relative prices, or price ratios, to review, are derived by taking the ratios of the n money prices in the system.

Moreover, as in Model A, the quantities of commodities demanded and supplied in Model B, the D_j and S_j, are quantities that enter the markets of the system reflecting how both Model A and Model B are market systems.

We shall form Model B's demand and supply functions by first setting out the system's interior or internal functions that we discussed in Chapter 2.4. Then we shall integrate these functions into Model B's demand and supply function.

We proceed to form Model B's internal functions by taking the ratios of the quantities of commodities demanded and the ratios of the quantities of commodities supplied; and we denote these ratios, which are each $(n-1)$ in number by r and s, respectively.

This, of course, requires measuring the quantities of commodities demanded (supplied) in a common unit in order to determine the ratios of these quantities. We show below Model B's interior or internal functions:

9. $\qquad r \equiv f(z)$
10. $\qquad s \equiv g(z)$

These interior or internal functions, functions (9) and (10), make the ratios of the quantities of commodities demanded, the r, and the ratios of the quantities of commodities supplied, the s, depend on the relative prices which are denoted by z.

We next use the interior functions $f(z)$ and $g(z)$ to form Model B's relative demand and supply functions. This is by entering these internal functions into the overall demand and supply functions of Model B.

We shall discuss in Sections 6.10 and 6.11 of this chapter how functions $f(z)$ and $g(z)$ can exist in Model B only because this system is rid of the incorrect or misused form of Say's Law that characterizes Model A. Model B's relative demand and supply functions are shown below:

11. $\qquad D_j \equiv F_j'[f(z)]$
12. $\qquad S_j \equiv G_j'[g(z)]$

Model B is characterized by the variable W which we shall temporarily leave implicit in the system. This variable, which was introduced in Chapter 1.6, reflects the system's overall output or income as well as the system's limited flow of resources.

Next, budget constraints arise in price systems because resources in the systems are limited. Hence the variable W in reflecting the system's limited flow of resources provides the basis for Model B's budget constraint. This means that the quantities of commodities demanded and supplied each sum to W.

We assume that these quantities are measured in a common unit, this being the unit in which W is measured. Let us now examine how the quantities of commodities demanded and supplied are each made to sum to W.

To review functions $f(z)$ and $g(z)$ determine the ratios of the quantities of commodities demanded and the ratios of the quantities of commodities supplied, respectively.

Functions $f(z)$ then operate on W to determine relative quantities of commodities demanded. Hence these quantities in being relative quantities adjust in a relative manner to always sum to W.

As well, functions $g(z)$ operate on W to determine relative quantities of commodities supplied. Hence these quantities in being relative quantities also adjust in a relative to always sum to W.

We noted that these quantities of commodities are measured in a common unit, this being the unit in which W is measured. However, the actual quantities, the D_j and S_j, are simultaneously determined; and these are shown as the dependent variables in Model B's demand and supply functions.

Clearly, these latter quantities, the D_j and S_j, are also relative quantities. This was established through our showing that these quantities, when measured in a common unit, always sum to W. This is only possible because these quantities, as measured in a common unit, adjust in a relative manner to always sum to W.

This implies that the actual quantities, the D_j and S_j, are also relative quantities. Let us now review a key facet to Model B that was sketched in Chapter 2.7.

Now the variable W also reflects Model B's overall output or income. Hence when we say that functions $f(z)$ operate on W to determine the quantities of commodities demanded that sum to W, we were taking or describing W as the aggregate demand for commodities.

Moreover, when we say that functions $g(z)$ operate on W to determine the quantities of commodities supplied, we were now taking or describing W as the aggregate supply of commodities. Consequently, Model B is characterized by Say's Law.

This is because functions $f(z)$ and $g(z)$ allow us to describe the system's overall output or income W alternately as aggregate demand and aggregate supply. This as was also discussed in Chapter 2.7 is a correct identity form of Say's Law since it is solely a descriptive device in Model B.

As well, individual quantities of commodities demanded (supplied) emerge from this correct identity form of the Law which ensures that Model B is wholly microeconomic in character.

This accounts for Model B as we shall discuss in detail in Chapter 9.7 being characterized by a correct form of Say's Law. This is a true identity that also acts as a budget constraint of relevance to microeconomics in a system.

6.4 Model B Is Consistent In Automatically Meeting The Counting Rule

We shall now develop the overall Model B which is our revised classical system. We proceed by using the system's demand and supply functions, functions (11) and (12) above to form excess-demand equations. These are equations (13) which, with functions (11) and (12), form the overall Model B that is shown below:

$$\textbf{Model B}$$

11. $\quad D_j \equiv F_j'[f(z)]$

12. $\quad S_j \equiv G_j'[g(z)]$

13. $\quad E_j'[f(z)-g(z)=0]=0$

Let us establish that Model B automatically meets the counting rule. We proceed by assuming that the system is in general equilibrium. This is reflected in the overall or external conditions $E_j'[\ ] = 0$ in (13) vanishing. This is only possible if the internal conditions $f(z)-g(z)=0$ simultaneously vanish.

Next, the latter conditions are $(n-1)$ in number hence they are just equal to the number of variables to be determined which are the $(n-1)$ relative prices, the z. As a result, Model B is automatically consistent in automatically meeting the counting rule.

We shall now examine why conditions $f(z)-g(z)=0$ vanish in general equilibrium which will allow us to bring out more fully the nature of the system's equilibrium conditions. When general equilibrium is established, the quantity demanded in every market across the system equals the quantity supplied in that market.

This also means that in general equilibrium, the ratios of the quantities of commodities demanded across the system equal the corresponding ratios of the quantities supplied across the system. That is, condition $f(z)-g(z)=0$ vanishes.

This condition, however, only implies general equilibrium because Say's Law holds in the system since the Law puts the aggregate demand for commodities identical to the aggregate supply. This explains why when general equilibrium prevails, conditions $f(z)-g(z)=0$ simultaneously vanish.

Next, these latter conditions, to review, are $(n-1)$ in number hence they are just equal to the number of variables to be determined which are the $(n-1)$ relative prices, the z. As a result, Model B is consistent in meeting the counting rule.

Moreover, this has been established without us having to impose Say's Law on Model B to eliminate a surplus equation as has to be done in the case of Model A.

Consequently, Model B is rid of the incorrect form of the Law that is imposed on Model A to ensure consistency of this system. This is an incorrect form of Say's Law because it is not a true identity.

This, to review, is because it is given the substantive role in Model A of ensuring consistency of the system. But the Law in being a true identity should not be given such a substantive role.

However, no such substantive role is given to the Law in Model B since it is not required to ensure that the latter system is consistent. This explains why Model B is characterized by a correct form of Say's Law which is a true identity.

This is reflected in the Law in Model B as we have established in Chapter 2.7 and confirmed in Section 6.3 of this chapter being simply a descriptive device in this system. Hence it cannot possibly be used to ensure consistency of Model B.

Neither can Model B's form of the Law restrict the system to long-run states. Whereas the incorrect Say's Law of Model A is used to make this system consistent; and as well, it restricts Model A to long-run states.

We have now set out Model B, our revised classical system. However, we shall carry the system a further step by bringing the variable W that is implicit in Model B, explicitly into the system.

This leads to a more detailed form of Model B to be referred to as Model B' which will assist us in bringing out the behavioral character of our revised classical system. In particular, we shall be able through Model B' to formally set out in detail the system's internal budget constraint.

Hence Model B and Model B' are both versions of our revised classical system with Model B' being only a more detailed form of Model B. However, we shall find that the less detailed form of our revised classical system, Model B, is more useful for some purposes. While the more detailed Model B' is more useful for other purposes.

6.5 A More Detailed Form Of Model B

We show below Model B, our revised classical system which we shall adapt to put into a more detailed form:

Model B

11. $D_j \equiv F_j'[f(z)]$

12. $S_j \equiv G_j'[g(z)]$

13. $E_j'[f(z)-g(z)=0]=0$

Model B, to review, is characterized by a limited flow of resources that we denoted by W but we left this variable implicit in the system. These resources provide the basis for the system's budget constraint. This means that the quantities of commodities demanded and supplied, as measured in a common unit, each sum to W.

Next, we discussed in Section 6.3 how functions $f(z)$ operate on the variable W to determine relative quantities of commodities demanded. Hence these quantities in being relative quantities, adjust in a relative manner to always sum to W.

As well, we discussed in Section 6.3 how functions $g(z)$ operate on the variable W to determine relative quantities of commodities supplied. Hence these quantities in being relative quantities also adjust in a relative manner to always sum to W. These processes as we also discussed in Section 6.3 brought a correct form of Say's Law into Model B.

Now we left the variable W implicit in Model B but we shall now bring it explicitly into the system. This is by entering W into Model B's demand and supply functions to form functions (11') and (12') of Model B' which is shown below. Hence W also enters the system's excess-demand equations, equations (13'):

Model B'

11'. $\quad D_j \equiv F'_j\big[W\{f(z)\}\big]$

12'. $\quad S_j \equiv G'_j\big[W\{g(z)\}\big]$

13'. $\quad E'_j\big[W\{f(z)-g(z)\}=0\big]=0$

Model B' as we have emphasized is simply a more detailed version of Model B hence both systems are forms of our revised classical system. Consequently, the systems are interchangeable and we shall use either of them as is appropriate for the analysis at hand.

We may also establish that Model B' like Model B is automatically consistent in automatically meeting the counting rule. As well, we discussed how conditions $f(z)-g(z)=0$ vanish when Model B is in general equilibrium.

Moreover, we have now brought out through Model B', which we also left implicit in Model B that the variable W also vanishes when conditions $f(z)-g(z)=0$ vanish.

This is now captured explicitly through condition $W\{f(z)-g(z)\}=0$ which formally reflects how there is a multiplicative relationship between W and conditions $f(z)-g(z)=0$. This, of course, explains why W vanishes with the vanishing of conditions $f(z)-g(z)=0$ in general equilibrium.

We have now set out in full detail through Model B' our revised classical system. General equilibrium of Model B' prevails when the overall conditions E'_j [ ] = 0 in (13') vanish. This, however, is only possible when the condition $W\{f(z)-g(z)\}=0$ within (13') simultaneously vanishes.

This latter expression is the internal budget constraint of Model B' which replaces Model A's external budget constraint form of Say's Law. Now W is brought into Model B' by the system's new aspect to behavior through functions $f(z)$ and $g(z)$. These lead to conditions $f(z)-g(z)=0$ which with W form the internal budget constraint of Model B'. That is, condition $W\{f(z)-g(z)\}=0$.

However, since Model A lacks this new aspect to behavior, hence lacking functions $f(z)$ and $g(z)$ and conditions $f(z)-g(z)=0$ of Model B', the variable W cannot possibly be brought into Model A's behavioral content. This causes W to be put outside the behavioral content of Model A by the system's incorrect Say's Law.

Then W in being put outside Model A's behavioral content forms the basis for the system's external budget constraint form of Say's Law. This external budget constraint, however, is not a correct form of Say's Law in not being a true identity; and it restricts Model A to long-run states.

On the other hand, the internal budget constraint $W\{f(z)-g(z)\}=0$ of Model B' as discussed in Chapter 2.7 and confirmed in Section 6.3 of this chapter, brings a true identity form of Say's Law into this system. This is a form of that Law that is simply a descriptive device that cannot possibly restrict Model B' to long-run states.

We have now fully set out through Model B', our revised classical system; and we shall now discuss why the system's new type of demand and supply functions were required in order to bring the aspect to behavior described in Chapter 1.4 into the system.

6.6 Why Model B's New Type Of Functions Were Required

We have discussed in detail how we have brought a new aspect to behavior into Model B, an aspect to behavior that is missing from Model A. This explains why we had to replace the orthodox demand and supply functions of Model A with Model B's relative demand and supply functions.

This is because these latter functions, unlike Model A's functions, reflect the new aspect to behavior that was described in Chapter 1.4. Now both Model A and Model B are characterized by the variable W that reflects the systems' limited flow of resources.

Next, the new aspect to behavior that we brought into Model B is first reflected in our taking individuals and firms to be aware that their resources, which we denoted by W, are limited. Let us now consider Model A then we shall return to Model B.

Model A, to review, is also characterized by the variable W. However, this variable is brought into the system by an incorrect form of Say's Law which leaves W outside the system's behavioral content.

Hence the W of Model A cannot possibly be the means whereby individuals and firms in the system are made aware that their resources are limited. However, Model B reflects how individuals and firms in this system are aware that their resources are limited.

This brings W from outside the behavioral content of Model A into the behavioral content of Model B where it reflects how individuals and firms are aware that their resources are limited. This is the first facet to the behavior described in Chapter 1.4.

Next, the new aspect to behavior that we brought into Model B also implies that individuals and firms, in determining their commodity demands and supplies, act in light of their awareness that their resources are limited.

This is to be ensured by individuals and firms determining quantities of commodities demanded and supplied that each sum to W.

This could not possibly be ensured by functions such as characterize Model A; since these functions account for an incorrect Say's Law being imposed on Model A with this incorrect Say's Law then putting W outside Model A's behavioral content.

However, the variable W as we have discussed is within Model B's behavioral content. We hence had to find functions that could operate on the W that is within the behavioral content of Model B in order to determine quantities of commodities demanded and supplied that each sum to W in this system.

This explains the rationale for the existence of Model B's internal functions $f(z)$ and $g(z)$ that we brought into the overall demand and supply functions of the system.

These internal functions, like W, are within the behavioral content of Model B. Hence these functions can operate on W that is also within the behavioral content of Model B to determine quantities of commodities demanded and supplied that each sum to W.

This is how we capture through Model B's functions the second facet to the behavior described in Chapter 1.4. Consequently, we have captured in Model B the overall behavior described in Chapter 1.4 since we have already captured the first facet to this behavior.

Finally, the quantities of commodities to which we referred are, to review, initially measured in a common unit.

However, the actual quantities, the D_j and S_j, are shown as the dependent variables in Model B's demand and supply functions.

6.7 Contrasting The Formal Structures Of Model A And Model B

Model A and Model B' are both characterized by the identical variable W that reflects the systems' limited flow of resources. Moreover, both systems determine identical quantities of commodities demanded and supplied, the D_j and S_j. However, there is a key difference between the systems.

Model A and Model B' both reflect consistency with limitation in resources, the systems hence reflecting the general logic of price systems. That is, the D_j and S_j in both systems each sum to W. This is ensured by the quantities of commodities demanded (supplied) in both systems being transformed into relative quantities demanded (supplied).

This is because these quantities, in being relative quantities, will each adjust in a relative manner in both systems to always sum to W. Let us now focus on Model A then we shall consider Model B.

Model A's functions first determine absolute quantities of commodities demanded (supplied). Next, the system is found to be initially inconsistent in that there is a surplus equation over the number of unknowns.

Economists then impose Say's Law on the system to eliminate this surplus equation to ensure consistency of the system. This transforms the quantities of commodities demanded (supplied) in Model A into relative quantities demanded (supplied).

This ensures consistency of the system with limited resources; since the quantities of commodities demanded (supplied), in being relative quantities demanded (supplied), each adjust in a relative manner to always sum to W.

This approach, however, brings inconsistency into Model A. This is because consistency of the system with limited resources should be ensured by the behavior in the system rather than by Say's Law.

Turning now to Model B' we find that this system's demand and supply functions, *in the first place*, determine relative quantities of commodities demanded (supplied). This is on account of the system's internal functions, namely, functions $f(z)$ and $g(z)$.

This ensures that Model B' from the outset reflects consistency with limited resources. As a result, consistency of Model B' with limited resources is ensured by the behavior in the system. Hence through Model B' we resolve the inconsistency of Model A.

This is because Model A's inconsistency, to review, stems from consistency of the system with limited resources being ensured as a result of the system being made consistent by Say's Law rather than by the behavior in the system.

6.8 Model B Reflects The New Aspect To Behavior That Is Missing From Model A

We shall now set out the overall rationale for why Model B', our revised classical system, reflects the new aspect to behavior that was described in Chapter 1.4. This new aspect to behavior, to review, is reflected in individuals and firms in Model B' being aware that their resources are limited.

Hence in being aware that their resources are limited, they act in light of this awareness; and they act in light of this awareness by determining quantities of commodities demanded (supplied) that each exhaust their limited resources.

This is ensured by individuals and firms in Model B' determining relative quantities of commodities demanded (supplied). Hence these quantities adjust in a relative manner to always exhaust the system's limited resources.

We shall now establish in detail that Model B' reflects this new aspect to behavior described in Chapter 1.4. This system is shown below:

Model B'

11'. $D_j \equiv F_j'[W\{f(z)\}]$

12'. $S_j \equiv G_j'[W\{g(z)\}]$

13'. $E_j'[W\{f(z) - g(z)\} = 0] = 0$

We have brought additional functions into the overall demand and supply functions of Model B'. These are the interior or internal functions, namely, functions $f(z)$ and $g(z)$. These functions determine only the ratios of the quantities of commodities demanded and the ratios of the quantities of commodities supplied, respectively.

Hence these internal functions in determining only these ratios of quantities cannot, on their own, determine the quantities of commodities demanded and supplied.

These interior functions of Model B' can only determine the quantities of commodities demanded (supplied) by operating on the system's limited flow of resources W. However, these interior functions are within the overall demand (supply) functions of Model B'.

As a result, they bring the system's limited resources W from outside the behavioral content of Model A, where it was put by the system's incorrect Say's Law, into the behavioral content of Model B'. That is, into the overall demand and supply functions, functions (11') and (12'), of Model B'.

This is how individuals and firms in Model B' are made aware that their resources are limited which is the first facet to the behavior described in Chapter 1.4. Next, individuals and firms act light of their awareness that their resources are limited which is the second facet to the behavior described in Chapter 1.4.

This second facet to the behavior described in Chapter 1.4 is reflected in individuals and firms determining quantities of commodities demanded (supplied) that exhaust their resources; and this is also ensured by the interior or internal functions of Model B', functions $f(z)$ and $g(z)$.

This is because these functions operate on the system's limited resources, that is, on W, to determine relative quantities of commodities demanded (supplied).

Hence these quantities, in being relative quantities, will each adjust in a relative manner to always sum to the limited resources of Model B'. This means that we capture in Model B' the second facet to the behavior described in Chapter 1.4.

Moreover, since we have already captured the first facet to this behavior in Model B', we have now captured the overall aspect to behavior described in Chapter 1.4 in the latter system.

Consequently, both facets to this behavior, and hence the overall behavior described in Chapter 1.4 stems from functions $f(z)$ and $g(z)$ of Model B'. Let us go further into this analysis.

Model B', to review, reflects the overall behavior described in Chapter 1.4 through initially capturing the first facet to this behavior. This is because W enters the behavioral content of the system to reflect how individuals and firms are aware that their resources are limited. Hence Model B' is characterized by the first facet to the behavior described in Chapter 1.4.

This awareness on the part of individuals and firms that their resources are limited then provides the rationale for the quantities demanded (supplied) in the system to be behavioral relative quantities demanded (supplied).

This is because in being aware that their resources are limited, individuals and firms are also necessarily aware that they must determine relative quantities of commodities demanded (supplied).

Since it is in determining relative quantities of commodities demanded (supplied) that they determine quantities of commodities demanded (supplied) that always exhaust their limited resources.

Hence to summarize our analysis, since individuals and firms in Model B' are aware that their resources are limited they determine relative quantities of commodities demanded (supplied).

This is because this is how they ensure that they determine quantities of commodities demanded (supplied) that always exhaust their limited resources. This explains why the quantities in Model B' are *behavioral* relative quantities.

This gives rise to functions $f(z)$ and $g(z)$ of Model B' to bring the second facet to the behavior described in Chapter 1.4 into the system. This is because these functions determine relative quantities of commodities demanded (supplied).

Consequently, these functions of Model B' determine quantities of commodities demanded (supplied) that always exhaust the system's limited resources which is the second facet to the behavior described in Chapter 1.4.

As a result, Model B' reflects the overall behavior described in Chapter 1.4; since we have already established that the system reflects the first facet to this behavior. This means that consistency with limitation in resources is ensured in Model B' by the behavior in the system.

Hence through Model B' we resolved the inconsistency we uncovered in Model A. This is because this inconsistency arises because Model A is made consistent with limitation in resources as a result of the system being made consistent rather than by the behavior in the system as is the case with Model B'.

6.9 Model B's New Aspect To Behavior Is Suppressed In Model A

We discussed in the previous section how functions $f(z)$ and $g(z)$ of Model B bring the new aspect to the behavior described in Chapter 1.4 into Model B.

However, these functions do not exist in Model A hence this new aspect to behavior is suppressed in this system. Let us, however, go further into this analysis.

Model A's incorrect Say's Law as we discussed earlier puts W, the system's limited flow of resources, outside the system's behavioral content.

Hence this variable, in being outside the system's behavioral content, cannot possibly reflect how individuals and firms are aware that their resources are limited. This means that the first facet to the behavior described in Chapter 1.4 is suppressed in Model A.

We may also readily see that the second aspect to this behavior is also suppressed in Model A. Say's Law, to review, puts W outside the behavioral content of Model A. Hence as we discussed, W cannot possibly reflect how individuals and firms are aware that their resources are limited.

This lack of awareness of individuals and firms in Model A that their resources are limited means that there is no rationale for the existence of *behavioral* relative quantities of commodities to exhaust the system's limited resources.

This is because it is only if individuals and firms are aware that their resources are limited would they be aware that they must determine relative quantities of commodities demanded (supplied). This is in order to determine quantities of commodities demanded (supplied) that always exhaust their limited resources.

Consequently, behavioral relative quantities of commodities demanded (supplied) do not exist in Model A to exhaust the system's limited resources. This then explains why functions $f(z)$ and $g(z)$ do not exist in the system.

Nonetheless, the quantities of commodities demanded (supplied) must be relative quantities in order for them to exhaust Model A's limited resources.

This, however, is ensured in Model A on account of the system's incorrect Say's Law being imposed on the system to eliminate a surplus equation. That is, to consistency of the system.

This as discussed in Chapter 1.10 ensures that the quantities of commodities demanded (supplied) in Model A are relative quantities demanded (supplied). Hence these quantities adjust in a relative manner to always exhaust the system's limited resources.

Clearly, however, these are not behavioral relative quantities. This results in $f(z)$ and $g(z)$ of Model B being suppressed in Model A to explain why the overall behavior described in Chapter 1.4 is suppressed in the latter system.

6.10 Say's Law And The New Aspect To Behavior Of Model B

We have discussed in Section 6.8 how Model B' reflects the new aspect to behavior described in Chapter 1.4; and this accounts for the system reflecting the general economic logic that should underlie all price systems.

We shall now establish that this new aspect to behavior could characterize Model B' only because the system is rid of the incorrect form of Say's Law that exists in Model A.

We discussed in Section 6.8 how within the overall demand and supply functions of Model B' are the internal functions $f(z)$ and $g(z)$. These functions determine only the ratios of the quantities of commodities demanded (supplied).

Hence these interior functions, on their own, cannot determine the quantities of commodities demanded and supplied. These interior functions of Model B' can only determine the quantities of commodities demanded (supplied) by operating on the system's limited resources W.

However, these interior functions are within the overall demand (supply) functions of Model B'. As a result, they bring the system's limited resources W into the behavioral content of Model B'.

This accounts for the W of Model B' reflecting how individuals and firms are aware that their resources are limited. We may now establish that this rids Model B' of Model A's incorrect form of Say's Law.

Model A's incorrect Say's Law had put the variable W outside the latter system's behavioral content. This meant that the W of Model A could not possibly reflect how individuals and firms are aware that their resources are limited.

However, the W of Model B' reflects how individuals and firms are aware that their resources are limited. This was accomplished through the internal functions of Model B' bringing W from outside the behavioral content of Model A into the behavioral content of Model B'.

Hence since Model A's incorrect form of Say's Law had put W outside the system's behavioral content, we rid Model B' of Model A's incorrect form of the Law. Let us put this analysis in the following way.

In order to bring the general economic logic of price systems into a system, we need to ensure that individuals and firms are aware that their resources are limited.

This requires that a variable such as W, in reflecting the system's limited flow of resources, be brought into the system's behavioral content as illustrated by Model B'.

Hence W, in being within the behavioral content of Model B', becomes the means whereby individuals and firms in this system are made aware that their resources are limited.

Next, the variable W must also brought into Model A; but this is accomplished by an incorrect form of Say's Law being imposed on the system to make it consistent.

This results in W remaining outside the behavioral content of Model A. Hence the W of Model A, unlike that of Model B' cannot possibly reflect how individuals and firms are aware that their resources are limited.

However, the behavior of Model B' brings W from outside the behavioral content of Model A into the behavioral content of Model B'. Hence the W of Model B' reflects how individuals and firms are aware that their resources are limited. This means that Model B' reflects the first facet to the behavior described in Chapter 1.4.

This, as discussed in Section 6.8, brings the second facet to this behavior into Model B' to account for this system reflecting the overall behavior described in Chapter 1.4. This results as discussed in Section 6.4, in Model B' being automatically consistent in automatically meeting the counting rule.

Consequently, we do not need Say's Law to ensure consistency of Model B' as is the case with Model A. This rids Model B' of Model A's incorrect form of the Law that is required to ensure consistency of the latter system.

This is then replaced in Model B' with a correct form of the Law that is a true identity. This is because the Law in Model B' is simply a descriptive device in this system as was established in Chapter 2.7 and confirmed in Section 6.3 of this chapter.

Hence Say's Law in Model B' cannot possibly restrict this system to long-run states. On the other hand Say's Law in Model A is not solely a descriptive device. This accounts for Model A being characterized by an incorrect form of the Law that restricts the system to long-run states.

6.11 Simultaneously Resolving The Inconsistency Of Model A And The Issue Of Say's Law

Model B', our revised classical system appears below:

Model B'

11'. $\quad D_j \equiv F_j'[W\{f(z)\}]$

12'. $\quad S_j \equiv G_j'[W\{g(z)\}]$

13'. $\quad E_j'[W\{f(z) - g(z)\} = 0] = 0$

We have brought the internal functions, functions $f(z)$ and $g(z)$, into Model B' to arrive at this revised form of Model A. Now for these functions to exist in Model B', they must have a role.

This role, which has already been discussed, is reflected in functions $f(z)$ and $g(z)$ operating on W to determine, respectively, the quantities of commodities demanded (supplied). These quantities, as measured in a common unit, each always sum to W.

Hence consistency of Model B' with limited resources is ensured in Model B' by the behavior in the system. This rids Model B' of Model A's inconsistency.

This is because Model A's inconsistency stems from limitation in resource being ensured as a result of the system being made rather than by the behavior in the system.

Consequently, it is on account of functions $f(z)$ and $g(z)$ that we rid Model B' of the inconsistency of Model A. However, as we shall now establish, functions $f(z)$ and $g(z)$ can perform this role in Model B' only because this system is rid of Model A's incorrect form of Say's Law. This, to review, is a form of the Law that restricts Model A to long-run states.

We have discussed how Model A's incorrect Say's Law puts the variable W outside the behavioral content of the system. Hence functions such as $f(z)$ and $g(z)$ cannot possibly exist in Model A since they have no role in this system.

This is because these functions cannot operate on the W of Model A to determine the quantities of commodities demanded (supplied). This is because the W of Model A is put by Say's Law outside the system's behavioral content. That is, outside the system's demand and supply functions.

Whereas the place of functions such as functions $f(z)$ and $g(z)$ as illustrated by Model B' is within a system's behavioral content. That is, within the system's demand and supply functions.

Hence since W is within the behavioral content of Model B', this means that we have rid this system of Model A's incorrect form of the Law; since this incorrect form of the Law puts W outside Model A's behavioral content.

We shall now discuss how W enters the behavioral content of Model B' which allows functions $f(z)$ and $g(z)$ to exist in the system. Let us, however, first review how the entrance of W into the behavioral content of Model B' allows functions $f(z)$ and $g(z)$ to exist in the system.

Clearly, the entering of W into the behavioral content of Model B' allows functions $f(z)$ and $g(z)$ to exist because this makes it possible for these functions to have a role in the system. This role is reflected in these functions operating on W to determine quantities of commodities demanded (supplied) that each sum to W.

This role of these functions in Model B' then accounts for the existence of these functions in the system. Hence we need to explain, as will now be done, how W enters the behavioral content of Model B' which, as discussed, will account for functions $f(z)$ and $g(z)$ existing in the system.

Functions $f(z)$ and $g(z)$ determine only the ratios of the quantities of commodities demanded and only the ratios of the quantities of commodities supplied. Hence these functions on their own cannot determine the quantities of commodities demanded (supplied).

They can only determine these quantities by operating on the variable W. However, functions $f(z)$ and $g(z)$ are within the behavioral content of Model B'.

Hence they bring W from outside the behavioral content of Model A, where it was put by Model A's incorrect Say's Law, into the behavior content Model B'. This rids Model B' of Model A's incorrect form of the Law. This is because this incorrect form of the Law had put the variable W outside Model A's behavioral content.

Consequently, the generality of Model B' is due to our bringing functions $f(z)$ and $g(z)$ into the system. These internal functions, as we discussed, account for us resolving through Model B', the inconsistency that we uncovered in Model A.

Moreover, we have now established that functions $f(z)$ and $g(z)$ could only exist in Model B' because this system is rid of Model A's incorrect form of Say's Law that puts the variable W outside the system's behavioral content.

This allows W to move into the behavioral content of Model B' which, as discussed, allows functions $f(z)$ and $g(z)$ to exist in the latter system; since these functions can now operate on W to determine the quantities of commodities demanded and supplied the system.

6.12 Say's Law And The Demand And Supply Functions Of Model A and Model B

We look in this book on demand and supply functions of a price system as arising from individuals and firms expressing quantities of commodities demanded (supplied) that are consistent with the system's limited resources.

This is reflected in these quantities demanded (supplied) in both Model A and Model B each always summing to W, the systems' limited flow of resources. These quantities in both systems, as we have established, are relative quantities; and this explains why these quantities always sum to the systems' limited resources.

This is because these quantities of commodities in being relative quantities, adjust in a relative manner to always sum to the systems' limited resources. Hence the demand and supply functions of both Model A and Model B arise out of the process described.

That is, the process whereby the quantities of commodities demanded (supplied) in both systems are transformed into relative quantities demanded (supplied). However, the relative character of Model A's functions does not have a behavioral foundation.

To review, we showed in Chapter 5.6 that the quantities of commodities demanded (supplied) in Model A are transformed into relative quantities demanded (supplied). This ensures that the system is consistent with limitation in resources.

This is because these quantities of commodities demanded (supplied), in being relative quantities (supplied), adjust in a relative manner to always sum to the system's limited flow of resources.

However, this transformation of the quantities of commodities demanded (supplied) in Model A into relative quantities demanded (supplied), as we also established in Chapter 5.6, is a result of the system's incorrect form of Say's Law being imposed on the system to ensure consistency of the system.

This restricts the generality of Model A's functions compared to Model B's functions. This is because the quantities in Model A should be transformed into relative quantities by the behavior in the system rather than as a result of the system being made consistent.

We shall now establish that this is the case with Model B'. Namely, that the quantities of commodities demanded (supplied) in this system are transformed into relative quantities demanded (supplied) by the behavior in the system. Model B', our revised classical system appears below:

Model B'

11'. $\quad D_j \equiv F'_j \big[W \{ f(z) \} \big]$

12'. $\quad S_j \equiv G'_j \big[W \{ g(z) \} \big]$

13'. $\quad E'_j \big[W \{ f(z) - g(z) \} = 0 \big] = 0$

We transform the quantities of commodities demanded (supplied) in Model B' into relative quantities of commodities demanded (supplied) by the system's internal functions, functions $f(z)$ and $g(z)$.

This is because these functions determine the ratios of the quantities of commodities demanded and the ratios of the quantities supplied, respectively. These ratios, with the variable W, then determine relative quantities of commodities in Model B'.

Hence functions $f(z)$ and $g(z)$ perform the same role in Model B' that the imposing of the counting rule on Model A performs in this latter system. This is the transforming of the quantities of commodities demanded (supplied) into relative quantities demanded (supplied). However, Model A's incorrect Say's Law is non-behavioral in character which restricts the generality of the system's functions.

On the other hand, there is a behavioral foundation for functions $f(z)$ and $g(z)$ of Model B'. This is because these functions, as discussed in Section 6.8, bring the new aspect to behavior described in Chapter 1.4 into Model B'.

This causes these functions to determine relative quantities of commodities. This, in turn, accounts for the functions of Model B', and hence the behavior in the system, ensuring consistency of the system with limited resources.

Hence through Model B' we resolve the inconsistency of Model A; since this inconsistency arises because consistency of Model A with limitation in resource is ensured as a result of the system being made consistent by Say's Law rather than by the behavior in the system.

6.13 Contrasting How Model B And The Keynesian System Are Rid Of Model A's Incorrect Say's Law

Model A reflects an incorrect or misused form of Say's Law since as we established earlier, the Law in the system is not a true identity. This is because it is given a substantive role in Model A. This is the role of ensuring consistency of the system.

Hence to bring a correct form of the Law into Model B, we need to bring a true identity form of the Law into the latter system. This also has to be done through Model B while preserving the latter system as a wholly microeconomic system. We discussed in Chapter 2.8 how this is accomplished through Model B.

To review, Model A's Say's Law brings a budget constraint of relevance to microeconomics into the system. This is because individual quantities of commodities demanded (supplied) emerge from this budget constraint to account for Model A being wholly microeconomic in character.

However, this budget constraint is brought incorrectly into Model A since it is brought into the system as a result of the system being made consistent by Say's Law rather than by the behavior in the system.

In contrast, as we discussed in Chapter 2.8, Model B's internal functions allow us to correctly bring a budget constraint of relevance to microeconomics into Model B. This is because this budget constraint is brought into the system by the behavior in the system.

This accounts for Model B, like Model A, being wholly microeconomic in character. However, Model A is restricted to long-run states by an incorrect form of Say's Law. On the other hand, Model B is rid of Model A's incorrect form of Say's Law. Let us now consider the Keynesian system.

Keynes also rid his system of Model A's incorrect Say's Law but in an alternative manner. This is by Keynes allowing the aggregate demand and supply of commodities in his system to diverge. This approach, however, results in the microeconomics of the real part of the Keynesian system being suppressed.

Whereas the approach in this book to ridding Model B of Model A's incorrect Say's Law accounts for Model B being wholly microeconomic in character. These issues will be covered in fuller detail in Chapter 9.

6.14 Why Say's Law Became A Problematic Concept In The Literature

Clearly, the issue of Say's Law restricting the orthodox classical system to long-run states is a deep-seated one which contributed to it being hidden and becoming a problematic issue in the literature. This is readily established. Three stages were required to resolve this issue through Model B.

First, we had to rid Model B of the inconsistency of Model A. Second, we established that in resolving Model A's inconsistency through Model B, we brought an internal budget constraint into the latter system.

Third, we established that this internal budget constraint reflects a correct form of Say's Law that is a true identity that cannot possibly restrict this system to long-run states.

On the other hand, Model A in reflecting the inconsistency we uncovered in the system is characterized by an external budget constraint. This is an incorrect form of Say's Law that is not a true identity and which restricts Model A to long-run states. We may also bring out in the following way why Say's Law became a problematic concept in the literature.

Economists rightly insist that price systems must be consistent; and they define consistency of a system to mean that the system must meet the counting rule. That is, that the number of independent equations and the number of unknowns must be equal.

Next, this counting rule is imposed on Model A by Say's Law which is used to eliminate a surplus equation from the system. Hence the Law ensures consistency of Model A by ensuring that the system meets the counting rule. However, the Law restricts Model A to long-run states.

Consequently, the Law plays a key role in ensuring consistency of Model A in ensuring that it meets the counting rule. Yet the Law also restricts the generality of the system by restricting it to long-run states.

This book has resolved this quandary in the following way. Model A, to review, is taken to be consistent in meeting the counting rule. Yet the system reflects the economic inconsistency we uncovered in the system.

Hence taking consistency of Model A to be ensured solely by imposing Say's Law on the system to ensure that it meets the counting rule is clearly an unsatisfactory approach to ensuring consistency of Model A.

However, Model A must be subject to this counting rule. This means that we must find a means other than Say's Law to impose this rule on Model A. Let us review how this was accomplished in this book.

This was through our uncovering and resolving the economic inconsistency that we uncovered in Model A through Model B. This was accomplished by our bringing the new aspect to behavior described in Chapter 1.4 into Model B. This new aspect to behavior is a substitute in behavioral terms for Model A's Say's Law.

This as discussed in Chapter 1.12 is in the sense that this new aspect to behavior ensures that Model B is consistent with limitation in resources. On the other hand, Say's Law ensures that Model A is consistent with limitation in resources.

Consequently, the new aspect to behavior that we brought into Model B not only rid this system of the inconsistency of Model A. This new aspect to behavior also ensures that Model B is consistent. That is, it ensures that Model B meets the counting rule.

Hence we do ensure consistency of Model B taking consistency of the system to be reflected in the system meeting the counting rule. *However, Model B meets the counting rule on account of the behavior in the system.*

This means that we do not need to ensure that Model B meets the counting rule by imposing Say's Law on the system; since Model B meets the counting rule on account of the behavior in the system. Hence we rid Model B of Model A's incorrect Say's Law that restricts Model A to long-run states.

Finally, we may bring out in another way why Say's Law became a problematic issue in the literature. Economists following Keynes recognize that Say's Law restricts the orthodox classical system to long-run states. They then usually attempt to resolve this issue by focusing directly on the Law.

However, as this book has amply demonstrated, Model A's incorrect Say's Law arises as a consequence of the inconsistency we uncovered in the system.

Hence we cannot possibly resolve the issue of the Law by focusing directly on the Law. Instead, we need to focus on what brings an incorrect form of the Law into Model A.

That is, we need to focus on the inconsistency we uncovered in Model A in order to bring a correct form of the Law into the system; since Model A's incorrect Say's Law that restricts the system to long-run states arises as a consequence of the inconsistency in the system uncovered in this book.

This is the approach we followed in this book through Model B. This allowed us to resolve through the latter system the problem of Model A being restricted by Say's Law to long-run states.

6.15 The Market Processes And Budget Constraints Of The Orthodox And Revised Classical Systems

We discussed in Chapter 1.6 how we broaden the meaning of the overall output or income of Model A and Model B W to also reflect the systems' limited flow of resources. Next, budget constraints stem from limitation in resources.

Hence the overall output or income of Model A and Model B will be the basis for the systems' budget constraints. Let us now focus on the latter system then we shall consider Model A.

Model B's overall output or income we shall find is determined by the system's behavioral market processes. This means that the budget constraint of Model B, in arising from the system's overall output or income, is also determined by the system's behavioral market processes.

Consequently, Model B's budget constraint is determined within the system by the system's behavioral market processes. Hence this internal budget constraint cannot possibly restrict Model B to long-run states.

Whereas Model A's overall output or income is determined in a non-behavioral manner. This is because it is determined by Say's Law through the non-behavioral market process we described in Chapter 4.2 rather than by behavioral market processes as in Model B.

This means that Model A's budget constraint, in arising from the system's overall output or income, is also determined in a non-behavioral manner rather than by behavioral market processes.

As a result, Model A's budget constraint is not determined within the system by behavioral market processes as in Model B. This accounts for Model A being characterized by an external budget constraint that restricts the system to long-run states.

On the other hand as we discussed, Model B is characterized by a budget constraint that is determined within the system by the system's behavioral market processes. Hence this budget constraint cannot possibly restrict the system to long-run states.

6.16 Review Of The Overall Rationale Of The Book

Model A the orthodox classical system is initially inconsistent in that it does not initially meet the counting rule since there is a surplus equation over the number of unknowns. Say's Law is then imposed on the system to eliminate a surplus equation to ensure consistency of the system.

This however, as we discussed earlier results in an incorrect form of the Law being imposed on the system that restricts it to long-run states. This is because Model A is made consistent by the non-behavioral Say's Law rather than by the behavior in the system.

Now it is Model A's functions and hence the behavior in the system that causes the system to be initially inconsistent. This then causes economists to impose Say's Law on the system.

Hence to rid the system of its incorrect Say's Law we need to look into the system's behavioral content. That is, into the system's demand and supply functions. It is in so doing that we came upon the economic inconsistency in Model A.

Next, as we shall now discuss, in resolving Model A's inconsistency through Model B, we rid the latter system of the Say's Law of Model A that restricts the latter system to long-run state.

Say's Law not only ensures consistency of Model A by eliminating a surplus equation from the system. We established that the Law also simultaneously ensures consistency of the system with limitation in resources.

This brought an economic inconsistency into Model A since consistency of the system with limitation in resources should be ensured by the behavior in the system.

However, we resolved this inconsistency of Model A through Model B by bringing the new aspect to behavior described in Chapter 1.4 into the latter system. This accounts for Model B automatically meeting the counting rule.

Hence we did not need the Law to ensure consistency of Model B. Consequently, we rid the latter system of Model A's incorrect Say's Law that restricts this system to long-run states.

This was replaced in Model B with a correct identity form of the Law that cannot possible restrict the latter system to long-run states. This means that Model A is restricted in generality compared to Model B.

Most generally, this is because consistency of Model A is incorrectly ensured in being ensured by the non-behavioral Say's Law. On the other hand, consistency of Model B is correctly ensured in being ensured by the behavior in the system. There is a further stage to our analysis.

As we discussed, through bringing the new aspect to behavior described in Chapter 1.4 into Model B we brought a correct form of the Law into this system. Let establish more precisely how this was accomplished.

Model B's new aspect to behavior brings a correct identity form of the Law into Model B. This is by bringing an internal budget constraint into the system. This internal budget constraint is a true identity form of the Law hence it cannot restrict Model B to long-run states. In contrast, the new aspect to behavior of Model B is absent from Model A.

This accounts for this latter system being characterized by an external budget constraint. This is not a true identity form of the Law; and it accounts for Model A being restricted to long-run states. In sum, much of the book turns on how consistency of Model A and Model B is ensured.

To review, Say's Law is imposed on Model A to eliminate a surplus equation to ensure that the system meets the counting rule. This very approach, however, brings an economic inconsistency into the system; since it accounts for consistency with limitation in resources being ensured in Model A in a non-behavioral manner rather than by the behavior in the system.

On the other hand, the new aspect to behavior of Model B ensures that the system meets the counting rule. This approach rids Model B of the economic inconsistency of Model A; since it accounts for consistency with limitation in resources being ensured in Model B by the behavior in the system.

Finally, we may confirm that Model B is rid of the inconsistency of Model A in the following way. This is through Model A being characterized by an external budget constraint form of Say's Law which is not a true identity; and this incorrect form of the Law restricts the system to long-run states.

On the other hand, Model B is characterized by an internal budget constraint form of Say's Law which is a true identity; and this correct form of the Law cannot possibly restrict this system to long-run states.

6.17 Summary

We developed our new type of demand and supply functions in this chapter, our relative demand and supply functions. These functions then provided the basis for our revised classical system, Model B, which was formally set out in this chapter. Then through Model B, we resolved the inconsistency that we uncovered in Model A.

Moreover, we established in Section 6.8 that this is because Model B reflects the new aspect to behavior that was described in Chapter 1.4. On the other hand, this new aspect to behavior as we discussed in Section 6.9 is suppressed in Model A which accounts for the inconsistency in the system.

We also discussed in the chapter how Model A's inconsistency led to this system being characterized by a budget constraint that is imposed externally on the system by an incorrect form of the Law. This is a form of the Law that is not a true identity and it restricts Model A to long-run states.

Model A's external budget constraint, however, is replaced in Model B with an internal budget constraint. This internal budget constraint reflects a correct form of Say's Law.

This is a form of the Law that is a true identity in being simply a descriptive device in the system. Hence it cannot possibly restrict Model B to long-run states.

Let us also review a key finding of the chapter which is that we simultaneously rid Model B of the inconsistency of Model A as well as of Model A's incorrect form of Say's Law. This was on account of functions $f(z)$ and $g(z)$ of Model B.

These functions rid Model B of the inconsistency of Model A. Moreover, as discussed in Sections 6.10 and 6.11, these functions could exist in Model B only because this system is rid of the incorrect form of Say's Law of Model A that restricts this system to long-run states.

This explained why these functions simultaneously rid Model B of the inconsistency of Model A as well as of the latter system's incorrect form of Say's Law. Then in Section 6.12 we reviewed the relationship between Say's Law and the demand and supply functions of Model A and Model B.

Next, in Section 6.13 we went further into how we rid Model B of Model A's incorrect form of Say' Law. Then in Section 6.14 we discussed why Say's Law became a problematic a concept in the literature.

In Section 6.15 we discussed the relationships between the budget constraints and the market processes of the orthodox and revised classical systems. Finally, in Section 6.16 we provided a sketch of the overall rationale of the book.

Chapter 7

Properties Of The Revised Classical System

7.1 Introduction

We have set out our revised classical system, Model B, through which we have resolved the inconsistency we have uncovered in Model A, the orthodox classical system; and in this chapter, we shall bring out some basic properties of Model B that stem from this system being rid of Model's inconsistency.

Both Model A and Model B, to review, are characterized by the variable W that reflects the overall output or income of both systems; and we also take W to reflect the systems' limited flow of resources. This means that W in reflecting the systems' limited flow of resources forms the basis for the systems' budget constraints.

Next, Model B is characterized by behavioral market processes that determine W in this system; and this means that Model B is characterized by an internal budget constraint that cannot possibly restrict the system to long-run states.

On the other hand, Model A's W is not determined by behavioral market processes; and this means that this system's budget constraint is not determined within the system. This accounts for Model A being characterized by an external budget constraint that restricts the system to long-run states.

We shall also establish in Section 7.4 that we may derive Model A from Model B. This will confirm that Model B has a more general character than Model A.

This is because reducing Model B to Model A requires restricting the generality of Model B. This is through removing from Model B the new aspect to behavior described in Chapter 1.4 that we brought into this system.

However, reducing Model B to Model A also implies that Model B is consistent with the maximizing behavior of individuals and firms that is the underlying basis of Model A. Yet Model B differs from Model A since unlike Model A, Model B reflects the new aspect to behavior described in Chapter 1.4.

This is because this new aspect to behavior that we brought into Model B is of such generality that it is consistent

111

with the maximizing behavior of Model A. We shall also discuss in Section 7.5 how Model B is wholly behavioral in character whereas this is not the case with Model A.

This is as would be expected since Model B in being rid of the inconsistency of Model A reflects the general economic logic of price systems. On the other hand, this general economic logic is suppressed in Model A on account of the inconsistency in the system.

Finally, in Section 7.6 we shall go further into the consequences for Model B of this system being rid of the inconsistency of Model A.

7.2 Model A's Restricted Type Of Market Processes

Model A is characterized by an incorrect form of Say's Law which is used to eliminate a surplus equation from the system to make it consistent.

This incorrect Say's Law, as well, brings a market equilibrating process into Model A, a process we described in Chapter 4.2; and this process ensures consistency of the system with limitation in resources. Let us review this process.

Say's Law puts the aggregate demand for commodities identical to the aggregate supply. Hence if there are excess demands anywhere in the system, these are matched by an equal excess supply elsewhere in the system.

Economists, drawing on long-run analysis, then conclude that the relative prices will instantaneously adjust to eliminate this disequilibrium in the various markets of Model A without changing overall output or income W. This accounts for W, the system's overall output or income being set at a long-run full-employment level.

This process, however, is of restricted generality since it stems from the non-behavioral Say's Law rather than from the behavior in the system. However, as we shall now discuss, this process is captured in Model B through the behavior in the system.

That is, Model B unlike Model A is characterized by behavioral long-run market processes that keep the system in long-run equilibrium but cannot restrict the system to long-run states. Whereas Model A is characterized by long-run market processes that stem from Say's Law. These imbed non-behavioral long-run market processes into the system that restrict it to long-run states.

7.3 Model B's Behavioral Long-Run Market Equilibrating Processes

We show Model B', the more detailed form of Model B, below:

Model B'

11'. $\quad D_j \equiv F_j'\big[W\{f(z)\}\big]$

12'. $\quad S_j \equiv G_j'\big[W\{g(z)\}\big]$

13'. $\quad E_j'\big[W\{f(z)-g(z)\}=0\big]=0$

To review, the variable W reflects the long-run full-employment overall output or income of Model B'. Next, functions $f(z)$ and $g(z)$ determine the ratios of the quantities of commodities demanded and the ratios of the quantities of commodities supplied respectively.

Next, as the z change functions $f(z)$ operate on W to determine quantities of commodities demanded that always sum to W. Moreover, as the z change, functions $g(z)$ operate on W to determine quantities of commodities supplied that also always sum to W.

Clearly, the quantities demanded in Model B', the D_j, are relative quantities. This means that as the relative prices change, these quantities demanded adjust in a relative manner to always sum to the variable W. We take these quantities and W to be measured in a similar common unit.

Next, the quantities supplied in Model B', the S_j, are also relative quantities. This also means that as the relative prices change, these quantities supplied adjust in a relative manner to always sum to W. We also take these quantities and W to be measured in a similar common unit.

Consequently, as the relative prices change, the quantities of commodities demanded (supplied) in Model B' as measured in a common unit each adjust in a relative manner to always sum to W.

This means that excess demands for commodities anywhere in the system are matched by an equal excess supply elsewhere in the system. As a result, the overall excess commodity demand (supply) is always zero.

This is a reflection of Model B' being consistent with the existence of long-run market processes. These are behavioral market processes since they stem from the system's demand and supply functions.

These behavioral market processes account for W being set in Model B' at a long-run full-employment level. Whereas W is set at long-run full-employment level in Model A on account of market processes that stem from the non-behavioral Say's Law.

Clearly Model A and Model B' are both characterized by market processes that ensure consistency of the systems with limitation in resources.

This is because these processes in both systems determine quantities of commodities demanded and supplied that each sum to W, the limited flow of resources of both systems.

However, as discussed in Section 7.2 this process in Model A is non-behavioral in character since it stems from Say's Law. On the other hand as discussed in this section, this process stems from the behavior in Model B'.

7.4 Deriving Model A From Model B

We first show Model A the orthodox classical system below:

Model A

4. $\quad D_j \equiv F_j\,[z]$

5. $\quad S_j \equiv G_j\,[z]$

6. $\quad E_j\,[z] = 0$

We also show Model B' our revised classical system below which is the system that we shall transform into Model A:

Model B'

11'. $\quad D_j \equiv F_j'[W\{f(z)\}]$

12'. $\quad S_j \equiv G_j'[W\{g(z)\}]$

13'. $\quad E_j'[W\{f(z)-g(z)\}=0]=0$

The relative prices the z influence the commodity demands and supplies in both Model A and Model B'. However, unlike Model A, the relative prices in Model B' influence these demands and supplies through the system's internal or interior functions. Namely, functions $f(z)$ and $g(z)$.

Moreover, it is through these internal functions that we brought the new aspect to behavior, and hence the general economic logic of price systems, into Model B'.

Let us now remove these functions from the demand and supply functions of Model B' while leaving the z as independent variables in these latter functions. Functions $f(z)$ and $g(z)$ as we discussed in Chapter 6.8 had brought the variable W into the demand and supply functions of Model B'.

Hence W is also removed from the demand and supply functions of Model B' with the removal of functions $f(z)$ and $g(z)$ from the system's demand and supply functions. This means that we transform Model B' into Model A.

However, Model A into which we have transformed Model B' is, as we have discussed earlier, initially inconsistent in an economic sense; and this also accounts for Model A being initially inconsistent in not meeting the counting rule.

Let us now follow the orthodox literature and impose Say's Law on Model A to eliminate a surplus equation which exists in the system. This is to make the system consistent. However, we established that this is an incorrect form of the Law.

This incorrect Say's Law then imposes on Model A the variable W that has been removed from within the behavioral content of Model B'. That is, W is now put outside the behavioral content of Model A where it forms the basis for an external budget constraint.

Individual quantities of commodities demanded and supplied then emerge from this budget constraint. This ensures that Model A is consistent with limitation in resources.

Such consistency, however, is ensured as a result of Model A being made consistent by the system's incorrect Say's Law rather than by the behavior in the system. This, of course, is the inconsistency that we have uncovered in Model A.

This inconsistency, however, has been resolved through Model B' on account of the new aspect to behavior that we have brought into the latter system. This is because this new aspect to behavior, as we established in Chapter 6.8, ensures consistency of Model B' with limitation in resources.

Hence through Model B' we resolve Model A's inconsistency; since this inconsistency of Model A stems from consistency of the system with limitation in resources being ensured as a result of the system being made consistent by Say's Law rather than by the behavior in the system

In sum, we have established that we may derive Model A from Model B'. This confirms that Model B' has a more general character than Model A. This is because reducing Model B' to Model A requires restricting the generality of Model B'.

This is through removing from Model B' the new aspect to behavior that we brought into this system through removing functions $f(z)$ and $g(z)$ from the system.

However, reducing Model B' to Model A also implies that Model B' is consistent with the maximizing behavior of individuals and firms that is the underlying basis of Model A.

Yet Model B' differs from Model A since Model B', unlike Model A, reflects the new aspect to behavior described in Chapter 1.4. This is because this new aspect to behavior that we brought into Model B' is of such generality that it is consistent with the maximizing behavior of Model A.

7.5 Model B Is Wholly Behavioral In Character

Individual price systems stem from the maximization behavior of individuals and firms which is behavior that is specific to each individual system. However, we shall now set out three general properties that are also needed to form consistent price systems.

These properties apply across all price systems hence they stem from the general logic of the systems. We shall then show that these general properties are ensured by the behavior in Model B.

This is as would be expected since Model B reflects the general economic logic of price systems on account of the system being rid of the inconsistency of Model A. On the other hand, we shall find that these general properties that are needed to form consistent price systems are ensured in Model A by the system's incorrect form of Say's Law.

This is also as would be expected since Model A does not reflect the general economic logic of price systems; since Model A's general logic, on account of the inconsistency in the system stems Say's Law rather than from the behavior in the system.

Now the three general requirements for a consistent price system to which we referred to are first, that the system should reflect the general economic logic of price systems.

That is, the system should be made consistent with limitation in resources by the behavior in the system. This is a new condition for consistency of a price system that is introduced in this book. Second, the system must solve for equilibrium quantities and prices. Third, the system must be characterized by market equilibrating processes.

We shall now establish that these three conditions are brought into Model B' by the behavior in the system. The latter system appears below:

Model B'

11'. $\quad D_j = F'_j [W\{f(z)\}]$

12'. $\quad S_j = G'_j [W\{g(z)\}]$

13'. $\quad E'_j [W\{f(z) - g(z)\} = 0] = 0$

We have established in detail that consistency with limitation in resources is ensured in Model B' by the behavior in the system. This means that Model B' reflects the general economic logic of price systems.

Next, when Model B' is in general equilibrium, the overall conditions $E'_j [\ ] = 0$ in (13') vanish. This requires that the term $W\{f(z) - g(z)\} = 0$ that is within equations (13') simultaneously vanish. This occurs on account of conditions $f(z) - g(z) = 0$ vanishing in general equilibrium.

Moreover, conditions $f(z) - g(z) = 0$ are $(n-1)$ in number hence they are just equal to the number of variables to be determined which are the $(n-1)$ relative prices, the z.

As a result, unlike Model A, Model B' is automatically consistent. This means that the system's equilibrium quantities and prices are determined; and this is due to the new aspect to behavior that we brought into the system through functions $f(z)$ and $g(z)$.

Next, functions $f(z)$ and $g(z)$ as we discussed in Section 7.3, bring behavioral long-run market processes into Model B'. This is through ensuring that the overall excess demand (supply) of commodities is always zero.

Consequently, the behavior in Model B' brings into the system the three general properties to which we referred that are required to form a consistent price system.

More precisely, it is the new aspect to behavior that we brought into Model B' through functions $f(z)$ and $g(z)$ that brings these properties that are required for a consistent price system into Model B'. Model A, in contrast, lacks the new aspect to behavior that we brought into Model B' through functions $f(z)$ and $g(z)$.

This, as we shall now discuss, accounts for the three general properties that are required to form a consistent price system being brought into Model A through the non-behavioral Say's Law rather than by the behavior in the system.

We have established that Model A is made consistent with limitation in resources as a result of the system being made consistent. This is by an incorrect or misused form of Say's Law being imposed on the system to eliminate a surplus equation.

That is, the system's general logic, as reflected in consistency of the system with limitation in resources, stems from the system's Say's Law rather than from the behavior in the system. That is, Model A does not reflect the general economic logic of price systems.

Also, since Model A is made consistent by the system's incorrect Say's Law being used eliminate a surplus equation from the system, this incorrect form of the Law allows us to solve for the system's equilibrium quantities and prices.

That is, Say's Law rather than the behavior in the system allows us to solve for the system's equilibrium quantities and prices. Next, Model A's incorrect Say's Law rather than the behavior in the system, as discussed in Section 7.2 brings long-run market processes into Model A.

However, these processes in stemming from Model A's incorrect Say's Law are non-behavioral in character. That is, Model A's market processes do not stem from the behavior in the system but from the system's Say's Law.

Hence to summarize our analysis, the three general requirements for a consistent price system to which we referred are brought into Model B by the behavior in the system. This means that Model B is wholly behavioral in character.

On the other hand, these three requirements for a consistent price system are ensured in Model A by the system's incorrect Say's Law. Hence Model A is not wholly behavioral in character unlike Model B which is wholly behavioral in character.

This is as would be expected since the three properties to which we referred stem from the systems' general logic; and the general logic of Model B is behavioral in character whereas the general logic of Model A is non-behavioral in character.

This explains why the three requirements for a consistent price system that we listed are ensured in Model B by the behavior in the system. As well, this explains why these three requirements for a consistent price system are ensured in
118

Model A by the system's Say's Law rather than by the behavior in the system.

7.6 Model A's Inconsistency Arises In The System's Behavioral Content

Model A's inconsistency stems from the system's general logic being ensured by Say's Law rather than by the behavior in the system. Model A's inconsistency, however, was resolved through Model B.

This is because this latter system's general logic is ensured by the behavior in the system. Hence Model B reflects the general economic logic of price systems. This accounts for the inconsistency of Model A being resolved through Model B. Let us go further into how this was accomplished.

Model A's inconsistency is economic in character since it arises because the aspect to behavior discussed in Chapter 1.4 is missing from the system. Hence Model A's inconsistency arises or exists within the system's behavioral content.

Consequently, to resolve Model A's inconsistency we needed to go into the system's behavioral content, that is, into the system's demand (supply) functions, and rid the system of this inconsistency.

This is by bringing the new aspect to behavior described in Chapter 1.4 into the system's demand and supply functions. Let us review in detail how this was accomplished through Model B' which appears below:

$$\textbf{Model B'}$$

11'. $\quad D_j \equiv F'_j \big[W \{ f(z) \} \big]$

12'. $\quad S_j \equiv G'_j \big[W \{ g(z) \} \big]$

13'. $\quad E'_j \big[W \{ f(z) - g(z) \} = 0 \big] = 0$

We brought the new aspect to behavior described in Chapter 1.4 into the behavioral content Model B' by bringing functions $f(z)$ and $g(z)$ into the system's demand and supply functions.

Hence through Model B' we rid the behavioral content of Model A of inconsistency by bringing the aspect to behavior that is missing from Model A into Model B'. This accounted for us resolving the inconsistency of Model A through Model B'. Let us now refer to Model A which appears below:

Model A

4. $D_j \equiv F_j [z]$

5. $S_j \equiv G_j [z]$

6. $E_j [z] = 0$

We have discussed how Model A's inconsistency arises because the aspect to behavior described in Chapter 1.4 is missing from the system's behavioral content.

This is reflected in functions $f(z)$ and $g(z)$ of Model B' being absent from Model A's behavioral content. That is, from the system's demand and supply functions. Hence the inconsistency in the behavioral content of Model A remains.

On the other hand, we resolved the inconsistency in the behavioral content of Model A through Model B'. This, to review, was by our bringing functions $f(z)$ and $g(z)$ and hence the new aspect to behavior described in Chapter 1.4 into the behavioral content of Model B'. That is, into the system's demand and supply functions.

This accounted for Model B' having a more general character than Model A which was reflected in various ways that were discussed in the book. Model B', for example, is characterized by the internal budget constraint $W\{f(z) - g(z)\} = 0$ that is within equations (13') of the system.

This is a budget constraint that cannot possibly restrict the system to long-run states. On the other hand, Model A is characterized by an externally-imposed budget constraint form of Say's Law that restricts the system to long-run states. Let us go further into this analysis.

We discussed in Chapter 1.3 how Say's Law ensures consistency of Model A with limitation in resources. This, however, brought inconsistency into Model A; since consistency of the system with limitation in resources should be ensured by the behavior in the system.

This, to review, is an inconsistency in the behavioral content of Model A. That is, an inconsistency in Model A's demand and supply functions. Hence we had to enter into the behavioral content of Model A to resolve the system's inconsistency.

This was accomplished through Model B'; since we brought functions $f(z)$ and $g(z)$ and hence the new aspect to behavior described in Chapter 1.4 into the demand and supply functions of Model B'.

These functions then ensured that consistency with limitation in resources is ensured in Model B' by the behavior in the system. Hence through Model B' we resolved the inconsistency of Model A.

7.7 Summary

We have set out our revised classical system, Model B, through which we have resolved the inconsistency we have uncovered in Model A, the orthodox classical system; and in this chapter, we brought out some basic properties of Model B stem from this system being rid of the inconsistency of Model A.

To review, both Model A and Model B are characterized by the variable W that reflects the overall output or income of both systems as well as the systems' limited flow of resources.

This means that the systems' overall output or income W, in reflecting the systems' limited flow of resources, forms the basis for the systems' budget constraints.

Next, Model B is characterized by behavioral market processes that determine the W in this system; and this accounts for Model B being characterized by an internal budget constraint that cannot restrict the system to long-run states.

On the other hand, Model A's W is not determined by behavioral market processes. This accounts for Model A being characterized by an external budget constraint that restricts the system to long-run states.

We then went into detail in Sections 7.2 and 7.3 concerning the market processes that are associated with the budget constraints of Model A and Model B. Next we established in Section 7.4 that we may derive Model A from Model B. This confirmed that Model B has a more general character than Model A.

This is because reducing Model B to Model A required restricting the generality of Model B. This is through removing from Model B the new aspect to behavior described in Chapter 1.4 that we brought into this system.

However, reducing Model B to Model A also implies that Model B is consistent with the maximizing behavior of individuals and firms that is the underlying basis of Model A. Yet Model B differs from Model A since unlike Model A, Model B reflects the new aspect to behavior described in Chapter 1.4.

This is because this new aspect to behavior that we brought into Model B is of such generality that it is consistent with the maximizing behavior of Model A.

We also discussed in Section 7.5 how Model B is wholly behavioral in character whereas this is not the case with Model A. This is as would be expected since Model B reflects the general economic logic of price systems. On the other hand, this general economic logic is suppressed in Model A.

Finally, we discussed how Model A's inconsistency arose because of an inconsistency in the system's behavioral content. This is because the aspect to behavior described in Chapter 1.4 is missing from the system.

Hence we had to bring this aspect to behavior into Model A's behavioral content. That is, into the system's demand and supply functions.

This was accomplished through Model B by our bringing functions $f(z)$ and $g(z)$, and hence this new aspect to behavior described in Chapter 1.4, into this latter system's demand and supply functions.

However, functions $f(z)$ and $g(z)$ and hence the new aspect to behavior described in Chapter 1.4, is missing from Model A's functions. That is, from the system's behavioral content. As a result, the inconsistency in Model A's behavioral content remained.

Chapter 8

The Keynesian System Bypasses The Inconsistency In The Orthodox Classical System

8.1 Introduction

We approach price systems in this book by dealing with the issue of how consistency of the general logic of the systems is to be ensured. That is, with how consistency of the systems with limitation in resources is to be ensured.

This approach led to Model B, our revised classical system, which has a more general character compared to Model A, the orthodox classical system. This is because unlike Model A, consistency with limitation in resources is correctly ensured in Model B in being ensured by the behavior in the system.

This as we discussed in Chapter 6.8 is due to the new aspect to behavior that we brought into the system. This accounted for Model B reflecting the general economic logic that should characterize all price systems. Model A and the Keynesian system, however, lack this new aspect to behavior hence this general economic logic is suppressed in these systems.

This, as we shall discuss in the chapter, restricts the microeconomics of both of Model A and the Keynesian system although in different ways; and we shall provide an explanation in this chapter for this difference between the systems.

This chapter and the following chapter will contrast Model B and the Keynesian system. However, we shall contrast only the general logic of the systems.

This is to bring out problems with the Keynesian system that arise because this system does not reflect the general economic logic that characterizes Model B.

More precisely, we shall contrast Model B and the Keynesian system to bring out problems with the latter system that arise because the system does not reflect the new aspect to behavior that we brought into Model B.

This means that we continue to adhere to the overall rationale of the book as spelled out in the preface. This is that we focus on the general economic logic of price systems rather than on the specific forms of behavior of individual systems. We do deal with the special form of behavior of the classical system. However, this was to assist us in bringing out the general economic logic that should underlie all price systems.

Finally, we note again that references to the Keynesian system in this book are solely to the real part of the system. This is the part of the system that deals with aggregate demand and supply variables.

8.2 The Keynesian And The New Approach To The Orthodox Classical System

Keynes, while uncovering that Model A is restricted to long-run states by Say's Law, yet left Model A untouched. This is reflected in Keynes in his system suppressing, rather than revising, Model A's microeconomic demand and supply functions as is done in this book.

This was through Keynes' use of aggregate demand and supply functions that suppress Model A's microeconomic demand and supply functions. Whereas through Model B, we generalized Model A's microeconomic demand and supply functions.

This was by transforming Model A's functions into Model B's more general microeconomic functions, our relative demand and supply functions. This, in turn, transformed Model A's incorrect Say's Law, which is an external budget constraint, into Model B's correct Say's Law which is an internal budget constraint.

This generalizing of Model A through Model B was possible because we uncovered and resolved through the latter system, the inconsistency that characterizes Model A.

This inconsistency, to review, arose because Model A does not reflect behavior that ensures consistency of the system with limitation in resources. This meant that Model A is subject to an unsatisfactory budget constraint since budget constraints arise on account of limitation in resources.

That is, the inconsistency of Model A concerning limitation in resources became reflected in the system's budget constraint. This explains why Model A is characterized by an unsatisfactory budget constraint, this being an external budget constraint that restricts the system to long-run states.

However, through Model B we resolved Model A's inconsistency concerning how limitation in resources is ensured in the latter system. This was by bringing the new aspect to behavior described in Chapter 1.4 into Model B.

Next, since budget constraints stem from limitation in resources, this led to Model B being rid of the unsatisfactory external budget constraint that characterizes Model A and which restricts the system to long-run states. This resulted in Model B being characterized by a satisfactory budget constraint which we described in Chapter 2.7.

This is an internally-determined budget constraint that cannot possibly restrict Model B to long-run states. Through this approach, we transformed Model A into Model B which has a more general character compared to Model A.

This is reflected, for example, as we discussed in Chapter 7 in Model B describing long-run states on account of the behavior in the system. On the other hand, as we also discussed in Chapter 7, Model A describes long-run states on account of the system's incorrect Say's Law which is not a true identity; and this incorrect Say's Law restricts Model A to long-run states. Consequently, we generalized Model A through Model B.

This is because Model B is not restricted to long-run states by an incorrect form of Say's Law, which is an external budget constraint, as is the case with Model A. This reflects how Model B is a generalization of Model A.

On the other hand, Keynes left Model A untouched and formed his short-run or macroeconomic system. Hence the Keynesian system is an alternative to Model A whereas Model B is a generalization of Model A.

8.3 There Is A Barrier To A More General Microeconomics In Model A And The Keynesian System

We have set out through Model B a new approach to price systems. This approach to price systems stems from the new aspect to the behavior of individuals and firms that we integrated into the system.

This is the aspect to behavior that we described in Chapter 1.4; and it brought the general economic logic that should underlie all price systems into Model B.

This new aspect to behavior that we brought into Model B accounted for our resolving, through Model B, the inconsistency that we uncovered in Model A. This, in turn, led to Model B reflecting a more general approach to microeconomics compared to the orthodox approach of Model A.

This means that Model A's inconsistency created a barrier to bringing a more general approach to microeconomics into the system. This is a barrier that arose because Model A lacks the new aspect to behavior that we brought into Model B.

Next, the Keynesian system also lacks the new aspect to behavior that we brought into Model B. Hence there is also a barrier in the Keynesian system to bringing a more general microeconomics into this system.

As a result, there is a barrier to arriving at a more general approach to microeconomics in both Model A and the Keynesian system. This barrier, to review, arises because both of these systems lack the new aspect to behavior described in Chapter 1.4 that we brought into Model B.

However, while Model A is restricted to long-run states, the Keynesian system can move among alternative states as behavior changes. Let us discuss what accounts for this difference between the systems.

8.4 The Keynesian System Bypasses Rather Than Resolve The Inconsistency In The Orthodox Classical System

We have discussed how the inconsistency in Model A created a barrier in this system to arriving at a more general approach to microeconomics in this system. This is because this system lacks the new aspect to behavior that we brought into Model B.

This, as we have established in detail, results in Model A being restricted to long-run states by an incorrect form of Say's Law which is an external budget constraint. Hence Model A's microeconomics is restricted to such states.

Next, there is also a barrier in the Keynesian system to arriving at a more general microeconomics. This is because this system also lacks the new aspect to behavior that we brought into Model B.

Yet while Model A is restricted to long-run states, the Keynesian system can move among alternative states as behavior changes, a reflection of the system's macroeconomic character. Let us discuss what accounts for this difference between the systems.

Through Model B we *resolved* the inconsistency that we uncovered in Model A. On the other hand, Keynes in the real part of his system *bypassed,* rather than resolve, the inconsistency of Model A. That is, the Keynesian system bypassed the barrier in

Model A to arriving at a more general microeconomics in this latter system. This was through Keynes shifting to his macroeconomic approach instead of approaching Model A through microeconomic analysis as is done in this book through Model B.

Then through the aggregate demand and supply functions of his macroeconomic system, Keynes suppressed Model A's microeconomic demand and supply functions that account for the inconsistency in the latter system.

This is how the Keynesian system bypassed Model A's inconsistency; since this inconsistency stems from the latter system's microeconomic demand and supply functions.

Hence the Keynesian system bypasses the barrier in Model A to arriving at a more general approach to microeconomics. This explains why the Keynesian system can move to alternative states as behavior changes. However, this is at the cost of the microeconomics of the real part of the Keynesian system being suppressed.

In contrast, we revised Model A's microeconomic demand and supply functions by transforming them into the more general microeconomic functions of Model B. These latter functions then accounted for us resolving, through Model B, the inconsistency of Model A.

That is, through Model B we resolved rather than bypass Model A's inconsistency. This also meant that Model B is not restricted to long-run states by Say's Law whereas Model A is restricted to long-run states by an incorrect or misused form of the Law.

In sum Model B like Model A is wholly microeconomic in character. But Model B, unlike Model A is not restricted by Say's Law to long-run states.

Next, Model B like the Keynesian system is not restricted to long-run states by Say's Law. But unlike the Keynesian system, Model B is wholly microeconomic in character.

Consequently, Model B partakes of properties of both Model A and the Keynesian system. This is reflected in Model B like Model A being wholly microeconomic character and in Model B like the Keynesian system not being restricted to long-run states by Say's Law.

8.5 Contrasting Model B And The Keynesian System

Keynes rid his system of Model A's incorrect Say's Law by allowing the aggregate demand and supply of commodities in his system to diverge. Keynes' aggregate demand and supply functions then determine an overall output or income variable that we denote by W. Let us now consider Model B.

This latter system is also characterized by an overall output or income variable that we also denoted by W. Next, Model B unlike the Keynesian system, is characterized by the new aspect to behavior described in Chapter 1.4.

We brought this new aspect to behavior into Model B through incorporating functions $f(z)$ and $g(z)$ into the system. This new aspect to behavior accounts for individuals and firms in Model B taking W to reflect their limited flow of resources.

This moves W from outside the behavioral content of Model A where it is put by the system's incorrect Say's Law, into the behavioral content of Model B where it forms the basis for an internal budget constraint.

This is a budget constraint of relevance to microeconomics since individual quantities of commodities emerge from it. This is on account of functions $f(z)$ and $g(z)$ of Model B operating on the variable W to determine individual quantities of commodities demanded and supplied that each necessarily sum to W.

These individual quantities of commodities demanded and supplied enter the markets of Model B reflecting how the system is wholly microeconomic in character.

Now like Model B, the Keynesian system is also characterized by a variable that we denoted by W that reflects the overall output or income of the system. However, the Keynesian system lacks the new aspect to behavior that we brought into Model B.

This means that individuals and firms in the Keynesian system do not take the Keynesian W as reflecting their limited flow of resources. Hence the Keynesian W is not brought into the behavioral content of the Keynesian system, to form the basis for an internal budget constraint of relevance to microeconomics as is the case with Model B.

This results in the Keynesian W, rather than individual quantities of commodities directly entering the Keynesian system's market processes with W being determined by macroeconomic or aggregative market processes.

This approach, however, accounts for the microeconomics of the real part of the Keynesian system being suppressed. We may also drawing on remarks in Chapter 1.6 contrast Model B and the Keynesian system in the following way.

Both systems are characterized by an overall output or income variable W which is a macroeconomic variable. However, this variable in Model B is also relevant to microeconomics since it forms the basis for the system's internal budget constraint.

This is on account of the new aspect to behavior that we brought into Model B. Individual quantities of commodities then emerge from this budget constraint and enter the markets of the system. This reflects how Model B has a microeconomic character.

In contrast, the variable W of the Keynesian system is relevant only to macroeconomics. This is because the Keynesian system lacks the new aspect to behavior that we brought into Model B that makes the W of the system also relevant to microeconomics.

That is, W cannot possibly form the basis for an internal budget constraint of relevance to microeconomics in the Keynesian system as is the case with Model B.

Consequently, the variable W of the Keynesian system, rather than individual quantities of commodities, enters the markets of the Keynesian system where it is determined by macroeconomic or aggregative market processes.

This reflects how the Keynesian system is macroeconomic in character whereas Model B is microeconomic in character. Yet while the Keynesian system and Model B differ in this way, there is a key similarity between the systems.

This is because as will be discussed in Chapter 9.11, both systems are characterized by internal budget constraints that cannot possibly restrict the systems to any specific states.

However, the new aspect to behavior of Model B ensures that this system's internal budget constraint is relevant to microeconomics to account for the system being wholly microeconomic in character.

On the other hand, the Keynesian system lacks this new aspect to behavior. This accounts for the Keynesian system's internal budget constraint being relevant only to macroeconomics to cause the microeconomics of the real part of the Keynesian system to be suppressed.

8.6 Remarks On How Keynes Bypassed The Inconsistency Of Model A

Model B and the Keynesian system are both rid of Model A's incorrect Say's Law that restricts the latter system to long-run states. This was accomplished in the case of Model B through our ridding this system of the inconsistency of Model A; since this accounted for Model B being rid of Model A's incorrect form of Say's Law.

Now the Keynesian system is not rid of the inconsistency of Model A. Yet Keynes' system, like Model B is also rid of Model A's incorrect Say's Law which restricts the latter system to long-run states.

That is, Keynes arrived at a similar finding as we did through Model B without Keynes resolving the inconsistency of Model A. This is the finding that the Keynesian system, as is the case with Model B, is rid of Model A's incorrect form of Say's Law.

We resolve the inconsistency of Model A through Model B using microeconomic analysis. This is through our bringing the new aspect to behavior described in Chapter 1.4 into Model B. We thereby rid the latter system of Model A's incorrect Say's Law. This accounts for Model B being wholly microeconomic in character.

Keynes, in contrast, rid his system of Model A's incorrect Say's Law through macroeconomic analysis. This is through Keynes allowing the aggregate demand and supply of commodities in his system to diverge. Hence we arrive at a similar conclusion through Model B and the Keynesian system.

This is that both of these systems are rid of Model A's incorrect form of Say's Law that restricts the latter system to long-run states. However, we accomplish this through microeconomic analysis whereas Keynes accomplished this through macroeconomic analysis.

This means as we discussed in the preface that Keynes' macroeconomics is, as it were, a short-cut to ridding his system of Model A's form of Say's Law. This, however, is a short-cut that is forced on the Keynesian system. Let us review why this is the case.

Through Model B we resolve the inconsistency of Model A; and in so doing, we came upon a more general approach to microeconomics compared to the orthodox approach of Model A. This more general approach to microeconomics allows us to rid Model B of Model A's incorrect Say's Law.

Hence through Model B we avoid Keynes' macroeconomic short-cut to ridding his system of Model A's incorrect Say's Law. This short-cut accounts for the microeconomics of the real part of the Keynesian system being suppressed.

On the other hand, we rid Model B of Model A's Say's Law through microeconomic analysis. This accounts for Model B being wholly microeconomic in character.

Consequently, we rid Model B of Model A's Say's Law while preserving Model B as a wholly microeconomic system. Whereas Keynes rid his system of Model A's Say's Law in a manner that accounts for the microeconomics of the real part of the Keynesian system being suppressed.

Now by focusing on the variable W we may readily bring out how Keynes bypassed the inconsistency of Model A. The variable W is imposed on Model A from the outside by Say's Law. This, however, accounts for the system being characterized by an external budget constraint that restricts the system to long-run states.

However, on account of the new aspect to behavior that we brought into Model B, the variable W moves from outside the behavioral content of Model A into the behavioral content of Model B. There it forms the basis for an internal budget constraint that cannot possibly restrict the system to long-run states. Let us now consider the Keynesian system.

As discussed, the variable W moves from outside the behavioral content of Model A *into the behavioral content of Model B.*

On the other hand, the variable W moves from outside the behavioral content of Model A *directly into the market processes of the Keynesian system where it is determined by Keynes' aggregate demand and supply functions.*

Next as will be discussed in detail in Chapter 9.11, the variable W forms the basis in the Keynesian system for an internal budget constraint that cannot possibly restrict the system to long-run states.

This reflects how the Keynesian system bypasses the process whereby W moved from outside the behavioral content of Model A into the behavioral content of Model B. This accounts for the microeconomics of the real part of the Keynesian system being suppressed. On the other hand, Model B is wholly microeconomic in character.

8.7 Further Remarks On Model B And The Keynesian System

We have discussed how Keynes rid his system of Model A's Say's Law in a manner that accounts for the microeconomics of the real part of the Keynesian system being suppressed. We may look on this problem with the Keynesian system as arising in the following way.

Keynes recognized that Model A is restricted to long-run states by Say's Law. Keynes then focused on ridding his system of Model A's Say's Law through macroeconomic analysis. This is by Keynes allowing the aggregate demand and supply of commodities in his system to diverge to rid his system of Model A's incorrect Say's Law.

This reflects how Keynes focused on a *symptom or consequence* of the inconsistency of Model A rather than on this inconsistency itself. This symptom or consequence of the inconsistency of Model A is the restriction of this system to long-run states by Say's Law.

However, through Model B we focus on Model A's inconsistency itself rather than on a symptom or consequence of this inconsistency; and we resolved this inconsistency of Model A through Model B using microeconomic analysis.

Consequently, we rid Model B of the inconsistency of Model A through microeconomic analysis to account for Model B being wholly microeconomic in character. Moreover, this accounts for Model B being rid of Model A's incorrect form of Say's Law which is hence accomplished through microeconomic analysis.

Keynes, in contrast focused on ridding his system of a *symptom or consequence* of the inconsistency of Model A. This symptom is the restriction of Model A to long-run states by Model A's Say's Law.

Keynes then rid his system of this symptom of Model A's inconsistency through macroeconomic analysis. However, this accounts for the microeconomics of the real part of the Keynesian system being suppressed. We shall go further into this issue in Chapter 9.13.

8.8 Summary

We reviewed in this chapter how we approach price systems in this book by dealing with the issue of how consistency of the general logic of the systems is to be ensured. That is, with how consistency of the systems with limitation in resources is to be ensured. This approach led to Model B, our revised classical system, which has a more general character compared to Model A, the orthodox classical system.

This is because unlike Model A, consistency with limitation in resources is correctly ensured in Model B in being ensured by the behavior in the system. This is on account of the new aspect to behavior that we brought into the system.

Model A and the Keynesian system, however, lack this new aspect to behavior. This, as we discussed in the chapter, restricts the microeconomics of both of these systems although in different ways; and we provided an explanation in this chapter for this difference between the systems.

This chapter and Chapter 9 bring out the primary consequences of the inconsistency of Model A for this system and the Keynesian system.

Model A's inconsistency results in this system being restricted by an incorrect form of Say's Law to long-run states. In contrast, the Keynesian system bypasses Model A's inconsistency. This causes the microeconomics of the real part of the Keynesian system to be suppressed.

This also means as will be discussed in detail in Chapter 9, that Keynes did not remove Model A's incorrect form of Say's Law from his system in a satisfactory manner. This is because Keynes removed Model A's incorrect Say's Law from his system in a manner that suppresses the microeconomics of the real part of his system.

On the other hand, we resolve the inconsistency of Model A through Model B. This accounts as will also be discussed in Chapter 9, for us removing Model A's incorrect Say's Law from Model B in a manner that ensures that the latter system is wholly microeconomic in character.

Chapter 9

Keynes Did Not Satisfactorily Remove Model A's Incorrect Say's Law From His System

9.1 Introduction

Keynes held that Model A is restricted to long-run states by Say's Law. However, we established that while Model A is restricted to long-run states, this is because of an incorrect or misused form of Say's Law that characterizes the system.

This incorrect form of the Law enters Model A because of the inconsistency we uncovered in the system. Hence to resolve the problem of Model A being restricted to long-run states by the system's incorrect Say's Law we need to rid the system of this inconsistency.

This is accomplished through Model B, this system hence being rid of Model A's incorrect form of Say's Law. Moreover, this is accomplished in a manner that ensures that Model B is wholly microeconomic in character.

Keynes also rid his system of Model A's incorrect form of Say's Law. This, however, as will be discussed in the chapter, is ensured in a manner that accounts for the microeconomics of the real part of the Keynesian system being suppressed.

Finally, we shall as we did in Chapter 8, contrast Model B and the Keynesian system. However, we shall contrast only the general logic of the systems. This is to bring out problems with the Keynesian system that arise because the system does not reflect the general economic logic that characterizes Model B.

More precisely, we shall contrast Model B and the Keynesian system to bring out problems with the latter system that arise because the system does not reflect the new aspect to behavior that we brought into Model B.

This means that we continue to adhere to the overall rationale of the book as spelled out in the preface which is that we focus on the general logic of price systems rather than on the specific forms of behavior of individual systems.

9.2 Remarks On Say's Law

Few concepts in economics have caused such problems as Say's Law, the "Law" that "supply creates its own demand."[11] We are referring to the identity form of the Law that appears in or is implied in various classical writings. Keynes and many other economists impute this identity form of Say's Law to the classical system.

This form of the Law, as discussed in Chapter 3.5, is represented by an identity between the aggregate demand and aggregate supply of commodities.

Becker and Baumol have referred to this identity form of the Law as Say's Identity.[12] However, we shall retain the term Say's Law to describe this identity since it is better known in the literature.

Keynes held that Say's Law is the "axiom of parallels" of the classical system; since to Keynes, given the Law, all the other properties of the classical system follow. Hence the Law, to Keynes, was what accounted for the classical system, which we represent by Model A, being restricted to long-run states.[13]

Economists have also shown that Say's Law gives rise to other problems with Model A. This is through the Law preventing money and market processes from being integrated into Model A in a consistent manner. This, in turn, invalidly dichotomizes the system into real and monetary parts.[14]

In fact, so problematic has Say's Law become that some economists have attempted to interpret the Law in alternative ways that imply that it is not a part of the classical system or that it is not an identity.

This has led to a conflicting literature on the Law. Patinkin, for example, in his *Money, Interest, And Prices* held that Say's Law is not a basic part of the classical system. Yet Patinkin also recognized that there is evidence that supports the contrary view that the Law is indeed a part of the system.[15] Other

---

[11] On Say's Law see J.B. Say, *A Treatise on Political Economy*, trans. by C.R. Prinsep (1834), pps. 138-39.
[12] G.S. Becker and W.J. Baumol, "The Classical Monetary Theory: The Outcome of the Discussion," *Economica*, XIX (1952), pps. 356-7.
[13] Keynes, *op. cit.*, Ch. 2.
[14] See Keynes, *op.cit.*, Ch. 3, Lange, *op. cit. (1942)*, pps. 49-68 and Patinkin, *op.cit.*, Ch.VIII.
[15] Patinkin, *op. cit.*, pps.193 and 645. See also Becker and Baumol, *op. cit.*, pps. 371-75 for a discussion that reflects how unclear is the literature on Say's Law.

conflicting views also characterize parts of the substantial literature on the Law, a literature we cannot cover in any detail here.[16]

However, attempts to interpret Say's Law to show that it is not an identity or that it is not a part of the classical system cannot satisfactorily resolve the issue of the Law. This is because we show in this book that the Law is, indeed, an identity or truism in our revised classical system, Model B.

This means that when properly interpreted, it can have no substantive role in a system. But Say's Law as we establish in this book became a problematic concept in the literature because there is an incorrect form of the Law in the orthodox classical system, Model A. This is due to the inconsistency that we have uncovered in the system.

This inconsistency led to substantive roles being imputed to the Law in Model A these being the ensuring of consistency of the system and ensuring that the system describes long-run states.

These invalid roles imputed to Say's Law in Model A brought an incorrect or misused form of the Law into the system; and this incorrect or misused Say's Law restricts Model A to long-run states.

However, in resolving Model A's inconsistency through Model B we rid the Law in the latter system of the substantive roles we described that are attributed to it in Model A. This accounts for a correct form of the Law entering Model B.

This as we shall discuss in Section 9.7 of this chapter is a true identity that also acts as a budget constraint of relevance to microeconomics. This is because individual quantities of commodities demanded and supplied emerge from this budget constraint.

This correct form of the Law, however, is missing from the Keynesian system; and this accounts for the microeconomics of the real part of the Keynesian system being suppressed. This, to review, is the part of the system that deals with aggregate demand and supply variables.

---

[16] For summaries of parts of this literature see, for example, Patinkin, *op. cit.*, pps. 645-50 and Becker and Baumol, *op. cit.*, pps. 355-76.

9.3 Resolving The Issue Of Say's Law

Overall, we may look on the issue of Say's Law as being resolved in this book through our showing that the Law in Model A suppresses an aspect to the behavior of individuals and firms in this system. This is the aspect to behavior that we described in Chapter 1.4.

However, we brought this aspect to behavior into Model B. Hence this latter system is rid of Model A's incorrect form of the Law that restricts Model A to long-run states. Let us go into this in detail through drawing on Model B', our revised classical system, which appears below:

Model B'

11'. $\quad D_j \equiv F_j'\big[W\{f(z)\}\big]$

12'. $\quad S_j \equiv G_j'\big[W\{g(z)\}\big]$

13'. $\quad E_j'\big[W\{f(z)-g(z)\}=0\big]=0$

Model B' as we discussed in Chapter 6.8, reflects the general economic logic that should underlie all price systems. This is because the system is characterized by the new aspect to behavior that we described in Chapter 1.4. However, this new aspect to behavior characterizes Model B' only because the system is rid of Model A's incorrect form of Say's Law.

To review, we discussed in Chapter 6.8 how within the overall demand and supply functions of Model B' are the internal functions $f(z)$ and $g(z)$. These functions determine only the ratios of the quantities of commodities demanded (supplied).

Hence these internal or interior functions, on their own, cannot determine the quantities of commodities demanded (supplied). These interior functions of Model B' can only determine the quantities demanded (supplied) by operating on the system's limited flow of resources W.

However, these interior functions are within the overall demand (supply) functions of Model B'. As a result, they bring the system's limited flow of resources W into the behavioral content of Model B'.

This accounts for the W of Model B' reflecting how individuals and firms are aware that their resources are limited. This, as we shall now discuss, rids Model B' of Model A's incorrect form of Say's Law.

Model A's incorrect Say's Law had put the variable W outside the latter system's behavioral content. This meant that the W of Model A could not possibly reflect how individuals and firms are aware that their resources are limited.

On the other hand, Model B' as we discussed reflects how individuals and firms are aware that their resources are limited; and this brought W into the behavioral content of Model B'. This was through the internal functions of Model B' bringing W from outside the behavioral content of Model A into the behavioral content of Model B'.

Hence since Model A's incorrect form of Say's Law had put W outside the system's behavioral content, we rid Model B' of Model A's incorrect form of the Law. Let us put this analysis in the following way.

In order to bring the general economic logic of price systems into a system, we need to ensure that individuals and firms are aware that their resources are limited.

This requires that a variable such as W, in reflecting the system's limited flow of resources, be brought into the system's behavioral content as illustrated by Model B'. Hence the variable W of Model B' becomes the means whereby individuals and firms are made aware that their resources are limited.

Next, the variable W must also be brought into Model A; but this is accomplished by an incorrect form of Say's Law, which is an external budget constraint, being imposed on the system to ensure that it meets the counting rule. This, however, results in W remaining outside the behavioral content of Model A.

Hence the W of Model A cannot possibly reflect how individuals and firms are aware that their resources are limited. However, the behavior of Model B' brings W from outside the behavioral content of Model A into the behavioral content of Model B'.

Consequently, the W of Model B' reflects how individuals and firms are aware that their resources are limited, the system hence reflecting the first facet to the behavior described in Chapter 1.4.

This, as discussed in Section 6.8, brings the second facet to the behavior described in Chapter 1.4 into Model B' to hence bring the overall aspect to behavior described in Chapter 1.4 into this system.

This as we established in Chapter 6.4, results in Model B' being automatically consistent in the sense that the system automatically meets the counting rule. Hence we do not need Model A's incorrect Say's Law which is not a true identity, and

138

which restricts the system to long-run states, to ensure consistency of Model B'.

This rids Model B' of Model A's incorrect form of the Law, this incorrect form of the Law, to review, being an external budget constraint that restricts Model A to long-run states. This incorrect Say's Law of Model A is then replaced in Model B' with a correct form of Say's Law. This is a true identity that cannot possibly restrict this system to long-run states.

This is because this correct identity form of Say's Law of Model B' is an internal budget constraint which explains why it cannot possibly restrict this system to long-run states. Let us draw on remarks in Chapter 1.6 to cover the preceding analysis in more detail.

9.4 Further Remarks On Resolving The Issue Of Say's Law

Model A on account of the inconsistency in the system is characterized by an external budget constraint that restricts the system to long-run states.

This means that this external budget constraint of Model A is not a true identity form of Say's Law; since were it a true identity form of the Law it would not restrict the system to long-run states.

However, in resolving the inconsistency of Model A through Model B, we brought an internal budget constraint into Model B. This is a budget constraint which, in being determined within the system, cannot possibly restrict the system to long-run states.

This means that Model B's internal budget constraint is a true identity form of Say's Law; since were it not a true identity it would restrict the system to long-run states.

That is, the fact that Model B's internal budget constraint cannot possibly restrict the system to long-run states endows it with the property of being a true identity form of Say's Law that cannot possibly restrict the system to long-run states.

On the other hand, the fact that Model A's external budget constraint restricts the system to long-run states results in it not being a true identity form of Say's Law that restricts the system to long-run states.

Next, it is because Model A lacks the aspect to behavior described in Section 1.4 that the system is subject to an external budget constraint. On the other hand, it is because Model B reflects this aspect to behavior that the system is characterized by an internal budget constraint.

Consequently, in light of the preceding analyses, it is because Model A lacks the aspect to behavior described in Chapter 1.4 that it is characterized by an incorrect form of Say's Law that is not a true identity and which restricts the system to long-run states.

On the other hand it is because Model B reflects this aspect to behavior that this system reflects a correct form of Say's Law that is a true identity and which cannot possibly restrict the system to long-run states.

This analysis brings out how through resolving the inconsistency of Model A we resolved the issue of Say's Law. This is because we resolve this inconsistency through Model B by bringing the aspect to behavior described in Chapter 1.4, which is missing from Model A, into Model B.

This, in turn, accounted for Model B as we discussed being characterized by a correct form of the Law that is a true identity which cannot possibly restrict the system to long-run states.

9.5 Alternative Approaches To Model A's Incorrect Say's Law

We discussed in the previous section how we have rid Model B of Model A's incorrect Say's Law; and we shall find it useful to contrast this with how Keynes rid his system of Model A's incorrect Say's Law.

An incorrect form of the Law enters Model A because the system's approach to microeconomics is restricted in generality. This is because Model A lacks the new aspect to behavior described in Chapter 1.4. This means that there are two ways in which we may rid a system of Model A's incorrect form of Say's Law.

We may generalize the microeconomics of Model A by incorporating into the system the new aspect to behavior described in Chapter 1.4. Alternatively, we may rid the system wholly of Model A's microeconomics.

Now the approach we follow in this book through Model B is to generalize Model A's microeconomics by bringing the new aspect to behavior described in Chapter 1.4 into Model B. We thereby rid Model B of Model A's incorrect Say's Law *while ensuring that Model B is wholly microeconomic in character*.

Keynes Did Not Satisfactorily Remove Model A's Incorrect Say's Law From His System

Keynes, in contrast, rid his system of Model A's incorrect Say's Law by wholly suppressing in his system Model A's microeconomics that accounts for the system being characterized by an incorrect form of the Law.

This was through Keynes resorting to macroeconomic analysis as reflected in his use of aggregate demand and supply functions. *This approach, however, results in the microeconomics of the real part of the Keynesian system being suppressed.*

Now our approach to ridding Model B of Model A incorrect Say's Law was possible only because through Model B we resolved the inconsistency of Model A; and this inconsistency was resolved on account of our bringing into Model B, the new aspect to behavior described in Chapter 1.4.

Moreover, this new aspect to behavior as we have established provides the basis for us to satisfactorily rid Model B of Model A's incorrect form of Say's Law. That is, to rid Model B of Model A's incorrect form of Say's Law while ensuring that Model B is wholly microeconomic in character. Let us go further into this analysis.

We rid Model B of the inconsistency of Model A through bringing the new aspect to behavior that we described in Chapter 1.4 into Model B.

Hence we generalize the microeconomics of Model A through Model B by bringing this new aspect to behavior into the latter system. Next, in generalizing Model B's microeconomics we rid the system of Model A's Say's Law.

Consequently, Model B remains wholly microeconomic in character yet the system is not restricted to long-run states by Model A's incorrect Say's Law. Let us now consider Keynes' approach to Model A and Say's Law.

To review, we removed Model A's incorrect Say's Law from Model B by generalizing Model A's microeconomics through Model B. This was by our bringing the new aspect to behavior described in Chapter 1.4 into the latter system.

Keynes, in contrast, removed Model A's Say's Law from his system by wholly suppressing the microeconomics of Model A in the real part of his system. This is through Keynes allowing the aggregate demand and supply of commodities in his system to diverge. Hence Keynes rid his system of Model A's Say's Law through macroeconomic analysis.

This means that the Keynesian system is not restricted to long-run states by Model A's Say's Law. However, the microeconomics of the real part of the Keynesian system is suppressed on account of Keynes' use of aggregate demand and supply functions.

9.6 Keynes Did Not Rid His System Of Model A's Say's Law In A Satisfactory Manner

Keynes held that Model A is restricted to long-run states by Say's Law. However, we shall establish that while Model A is indeed restricted to long-run states, this is because the system is characterized by an incorrect or misused form of the Law; and it is this incorrect Say's Law that restricts Model A to long-run states.

Economists in setting out Model A write Say's Law as an identity. However, this identity is misused in Model A in being given the substantive role in Model A of eliminating a surplus equation to ensure consistency of the system. That is, that the system meet the counting rule.

This explains why we concluded that there is an incorrect or misused form of the Law in Model A; since a correct form of the Law should not be given the substantive role described.

Now we recognize in this book that Model A is characterized by an incorrect form of Say's Law that accounts for the system being restricted to long-run states. Hence the solution to this is to bring a correct form of the Law into Model A.

Keynes, in contrast, wholly removed Model A's incorrect Say's Law from his system. This was through Keynes allowing the aggregate demand and supply of commodities in his system to diverge. We shall now discuss the consequences of this for the Keynesian system.

Let us focus on two properties that stem from Model A's incorrect Say's Law. First, it restricts Model A to long-run states. Second, it forms the basis for a budget constraint of relevance to microeconomics.

This is because individual quantities of commodities demanded (supplied) emerge from this budget constraint. This accounts for Model A being wholly microeconomic in character.

Hence Keynes in wholly ridding his system of Model A's incorrect Say's Law, rid his system of both of the properties that we described stem from Model A's Say's Law.

Consequently, the Keynesian system in being rid of the first property of Model A's incorrect Say's Law, can move to alternative states as behavior changes; since it is not restricted to long-run states by Model A's incorrect Say's Law.

Keynes Did Not Satisfactorily Remove Model A's Incorrect Say's Law From His System

Keynes, however, simultaneously rid his system of the second property of Model A's incorrect Say's Law. This is the property that is reflected in Say's Law providing the basis in Model A for a budget constraint of relevance to microeconomics.

Keynes' ridding his system of this second property of Model A's incorrect Say's Law accounts for the microeconomics of the real part of the Keynesian system being suppressed. Let us now consider Model B.

We rid Model B of Model A's incorrect Say's Law by transforming this incorrect Say's Law from being an externally-imposed budget constraint into an internal budget constraint in Model B.

This internal budget constraint of Model B replaces Model A's incorrect Say's Law which is not a true identity with a true identity form of the Law. Hence Model B like the Keynesian system is not restricted to long-run states by Model A's incorrect Say's Law.

However, we do not rid Model B of the second property of Model A's incorrect Say's Law. This is the property reflected in Model A's incorrect Say's Law providing the basis for a budget constraint of relevance to microeconomics in the system.

Instead, we bring this property correctly into Model B through this system's internal budget constraint since this budget constraint stems from the behavior in the system; and this internal budget constraint is of relevance to microeconomics since individual quantities of commodities emerge from it.

Whereas Model A's budget constraint that is also of relevance to microeconomics enters the system as a result of Say's Law being imposed on the system to ensure consistency of the system.

Hence to summarize our analysis, Keynes did not rid his system of Model A's incorrect Say's Law in a satisfactory manner; since this is accomplished in a manner that accounts for the microeconomics of the Keynesian system being suppressed.

On the other hand, we rid Model B of Model A's incorrect Say's Law in a manner that ensures that Model B is wholly microeconomic in character. We can now bring out a basic issue with how Keynes approached the classical system and Say's Law.

Now the orthodox classical system, Model A, is restricted to long-run states by Say's Law, a form of the Law which we established is an incorrect or misused form of the Law. Keynes then wholly removed Model A's incorrect Say's Law from his system.

This means that the Keynesian system is not restricted by Model A's Say's Law to long-run states hence it can move to alternative states as behavior changes, a reflection of the system's macroeconomic character.

However, while Model A's incorrect Say's Law does indeed restrict the system to long-run states the solution to this is not simply to rid this system of this incorrect form of the Law. We need to ask the question of why, in the first place, an incorrect form of the Law entered Model A?

Through pursuing this question, we uncovered that an incorrect form of Say's Law entered Model A because of the inconsistency we uncovered in the system.

This inconsistency arose because Model A lacks the new aspect to behavior described in Chapter 1.4. However, we brought this new aspect behavior into Model B. Hence through the latter system, we resolved the inconsistency of Model A.

This accounted for Model B being rid of Model A's incorrect Say's Law in a manner that ensured that Model B is wholly microeconomic in character. On the other hand, Keynes rid his system of Model A's Say's Law in a manner that resulted in the microeconomics of the real part of the Keynesian system being suppressed.

9.7 The True Nature of Say's Law

We shall be able to isolate the true nature of Say's Law by first examining a key role that Model A's incorrect Say's Law plays in this system. Then we shall bring out how this role is ensured in Model B by a form of the Law which, as we shall establish, reflects the true nature of Say's Law.

Model A's incorrect Say's Law imposes on the system the variable W that reflects the system's limited flow of resources. However, this variable is put outside Model A's behavioral content by the system's incorrect Say's Law.

Next, the system is made consistent by this incorrect form of the Law being used to eliminate a surplus equation from the system. This ensures that the quantities of commodities demanded (supplied) each sum to W.

This means that Say's Law in imposing W on Model A subjects the system to an external budget constraint. This is a budget constraint of relevance to microeconomics. This is because individual quantities of commodities demanded (supplied) emerge from this budget constraint and enter the markets of Model A.

Now in ridding Model A of its incorrect form of the Law through Model B, we rid the latter system of this external budget constraint of Model A. This is because Model A's external budget constraint is transformed in Model B into an internal budget constraint.

This internal budget constraint as we established in Chapter 2.7 and confirmed in Chapter 6.3, reflects a true identity form of Say's Law; and it is the means whereby we rid Model B of Model A's external budget constraint and hence of Model A's incorrect Say's Law, a form of the Law that is not a true identity.

Consequently, Model B reflects a correct form of the Law that is a true identity. Moreover, this correct or true identity form of the Law also acts in Model B as a budget constraint of relevance to microeconomics.

This is because individual quantities of commodities demanded (supplied) emerge from this budget constraint and enter the system's markets.

We can now drawing on Model B bring out the correct nature of Say's Law: *this is a true identity that also acts as a budget constraint of relevance to microeconomics in a system.* Hence there are two conditions that must both be met for a system to reflect a correct form of Say's Law.

That is, the Law must be a true identity and it must also act as a budget constraint of relevance to microeconomics. This is in the sense that individual quantities of commodities demanded (supplied) must emerge from this budget constraint.

We shall now examine Model A and the Keynesian system to see whether or not they reflect both of these conditions that are required to bring a true or correct Say's Law into a system. Let us first consider Model A with the Keynesian system being considered in the following section.

Say's Law is not a true identity in Model A since it is given a substantive role in the system. This is the role of ensuring consistency of the system.

However, it acts as a budget constraint of relevance to microeconomics since individual quantities of commodities emerge from it. This ensures that Model A is wholly microeconomic in character.

Hence Model A does not reflect both of the conditions that are required to bring a true or correct form of Say's Law into a system since Model A reflects only one of these conditions. This explains why Model A is characterized by an incorrect form of

Say's Law that restricts the system to long-run states. Let us now consider the Keynesian system.

9.8 Keynes' Approach To Model A's Incorrect Say's Law

Keynes removed Model A's incorrect or misused form of Say's Law from his system by allowing the aggregate demand and supply of commodities in his system to diverge to determine an overall output or income variable.

This brings a property into the Keynesian system that is equivalent to bringing a true identity form of the Law into the system. This is because Keynes' allowing the aggregate demand and supply of commodities in his system to diverge means that his system is not restricted by Say's Law to long-run states.

Moreover, were we to bring a true identity form of the Law into the Keynesian system this would also ensure that the system is not restricted by the Law to long-run states.

However, we shall find that Keynes' approach to ridding his system of Model A's incorrect Say's Law by allowing the aggregate demand and supply of commodities to diverge is not a satisfactory approach.

This is because it results in the microeconomics of the real part of the Keynesian system being suppressed. Let us establish this in detail.

We recognize in this book that Model A is characterized by an incorrect form of Say's Law that accounts for the system being restricted to long-run states. This means that the solution to this is to replace Model A's incorrect Say's Law with a correct form of the Law.

Keynes instead completely removed Model A's incorrect Say's Law from his system. This was through Keynes allowing the aggregate demand and supply of commodities in his system to diverge. However, we recognize in this book that Model A reflects an incorrect form of Say's Law.

This means as we discussed, that the solution to this is to bring a correct form of the Law into Model B rather than wholly ridding this system of Model A's incorrect Say's Law. We accomplished this through the new aspect to behavior that we brought into Model B.

Hence unlike the Keynesian system, Model B remains characterized by Say's Law but a correct form of the Law that is a true identity that cannot possibly restrict the system to long-run states. Moreover, Model B's correct Say's Law brought a key property into the system.

This as we established in Chapter 2.8, is reflected in Model B being characterized by an internal budget constraint of relevance to microeconomics that stems from the behavior in the system. Individual quantities of commodities demanded (supplied) then emerge from this budget constraint which accounts for Model B being wholly microeconomic in character.

Keynes, in contrast, completely rid his system of Model A's incorrect Say's Law that restricts the latter system to long-run states. Hence Keynes' system is not restricted by the Law to long-run states.

Keynes, however, in ridding his system wholly of Model A's incorrect Say's Law, thereby also rid his system of the key property of Model A's incorrect Say's Law to which we have referred.

This property, to review, is reflected in Model A's incorrect Say's Law providing the basis for a budget constraint in the system of relevance to microeconomics in that individual quantities of commodities demanded (supplied) emerge from this budget constraint.

Hence Keynes in ridding his system wholly of Model A's incorrect Say's Law also rid his system of this key property of Model A's incorrect Say's Law.

Consequently, this property is missing from the Keynesian system which accounts for the microeconomics of the real part of the system being suppressed. This means that the Keynesian system is not characterized by a correct form of Say's Law.

This is because the Keynesian system does not reflect the second condition for a correct form of the Law that was set out in the previous section. This, to review, is that a correct form of the Law should also act as a budget constraint of relevance to microeconomics in a system.

9.9 Contrasting The General Logic Of Model B And The Keynesian System

Clearly, the Keynesian system does not reflect the new aspect to behavior described in Chapter 1.4 that we brought into Model B. This is because functions of the general type of functions $f(z)$ and $g(z)$ that characterize Model B are absent from the

Keynesian system. These functions, to review, bring the variable W from outside the behavioral content of Model A, where it is put by system's incorrect Say's Law, into the behavioral content of Model B.

Moreover, functions $f(z)$ and $g(z)$ of Model B operate on W to determine individual quantities of commodities demanded (supplied) that enter the markets of Model B.

This accounts as we discussed in Chapter 2.7 and confirmed in Chapter 6.3, for Model B being characterized by a true identity form of Say's Law. As well, this true identity form of Say's Law is a budget constraint of relevance to microeconomics in the system.

This is because individual quantities of commodities demanded (supplied) emerge from this budget constraint to account for Model B being wholly microeconomic in character.

Consequently, Model B reflects a true or correct form of Say's Law since the system meets both of the conditions discussed in Section 9.7 that are required for such a true form of the Law to characterize a system.

Now Keynes held that Model A is restricted to long-run states by Say's Law. This immediately tells us that Keynes was referring to an incorrect form of the Law. This is because Say's Law in being a true identity should not have any influence in Model A.

Hence we must focus on ridding Model A of its incorrect Say's Law, which is not a true identity, and replacing it with a true identity form of the Law rather than completely ridding the system of its incorrect form of Say's Law as Keynes did through his macroeconomic analysis.

Moreover, this must be done in a manner that maintains through Model B the basic character of Model A as a wholly microeconomic system. This was accomplished by our ridding Model A through Model B of the inconsistency we uncovered in Model A.

To review, we resolved this inconsistency through Model B by our bringing the new aspect to behavior described in Chapter 1.4 into Model B through functions $f(z)$ and $g(z)$. These functions accounted for our ridding Model B of Model A's incorrect Say's Law which is not a true identity.

Model A's incorrect Say's Law was then replaced with a correct form of the Law in Model B. This is a true identity that cannot possibly restrict this latter system to long-run states. Moreover, Model B's true identity form of the Law provides the basis for a budget constraint of relevance to microeconomics. This
148

is because individual quantities of commodities emerge from this budget constraint. This accounts for Model B being wholly microeconomic in character.

Hence through Model B we resolved the problem of Model A being restricted to long-run states by Say's Law. Moreover, this was accomplished while maintaining Model B as a wholly microeconomic system.

Keynes also rid his system of Model A incorrect Say's Law but this was by Keynes allowing the aggregate demand and supply of commodities in his macroeconomic system to diverge.

Keynes, however, thereby also rid his system of the property reflected in Model A's incorrect Say's Law that provides the basis for a budget constraint of relevance to microeconomics in the latter system.

Hence Keynes in ridding his system wholly of Model A's incorrect Say's Law also rid his system of this key property of Model A's incorrect Say's Law. Consequently, this property is missing from the Keynesian system which accounts for the microeconomics of the real part of the system being suppressed.

In contrast, we did not rid Model B of the property of Model A's incorrect Say's Law of providing the basis for a budget constraint in the system of relevance to microeconomics. Instead, we brought this property correctly into Model B.

This is because we brought this property into Model B through the behavior of the system rather than through Say's Law. This accounts for Model B, unlike the Keynesian system, being wholly microeconomic in character.

9.10 Model A, Model B And The Keynesian System

We show Model B' our revised classical system below:

$$\textbf{Model B'}$$

$$11'. \quad D_j \equiv F_j'\big[W\{f(z)\}\big]$$

$$12'. \quad S_j \equiv G_j'\big[W\{g(z)\}\big]$$

$$13'. \quad E_j'\big[W\{f(z)-g(z)\}=0\big]=0$$

General equilibrium of Model B' prevails when the overall condition $E_j'\,[\;] = 0$ in (13') vanishes. This is only possible were the internal condition $W\{f(z)-g(z)\}=0$ to simultaneously vanish.

This expression that is within equations (13') is, to review, the internal budget constraint of Model B' which replaces Model A's external budget constraint form of Say's Law.

Now W is brought into Model B' by functions $f(z)$ and $g(z)$ that bring the new aspect to behavior described in Chapter 1.4 into the system. These functions lead to condition $f(z)-g(z)\neq0$ which with W gives rise to the system's internal budget constraint. Namely, expression $W\{f(z)-g(z)\}=0$.

On the other hand, Model A lacks this new aspect to behavior, hence lacking functions $f(z)$ and $g(z)$ and condition $f(z)-g(z)\neq0$. Hence W could not possibly be brought into the behavioral content of Model A. This results in W being put outside the behavioral content of Model A where it forms the basis for the system's external budget constraint.

This external budget constraint is not a correct form of Say's Law in not being a true identity; and it restricts Model A to long-run states. However, there is another property of Model A's incorrect Say's Law to be considered.

This is because Model A's incorrect Say's Law also forms the basis for a budget constraint of relevance to microeconomics; since individual quantities of commodities demanded (supplied) emerge from this budget constraint. This gives Model A a wholly microeconomic character.

We can now bring out the consequences for Model B' of the new aspect to behavior of that we brought into this system. This new aspect to behavior of Model B' rids this system *only* of the property of Model A's incorrect Say's Law that restricts the system to long-run states.

This, of course, explains why through Model B' we resolve the issue of Model A being restricted to long-run states. Yet we preserve in Model B' the key property of Model A's incorrect Say's Law of providing the basis in the system for a budget constraint of relevance to microeconomics. This accounts for Model B' being wholly microeconomic in character.

This is because rather than ridding Model B' of this property, we brought it correctly into Model B' through bringing it into the system through the behavior in the system rather than through Say's Law as is the case with Model A.

Now Model A's incorrect Say's Law as discussed provides the basis for a budget constraint of relevance to microeconomics in the system. This accounts for Model A being wholly microeconomic in character although the system is restricted to long-run states by its incorrect form of Say's Law.

Keynes then wholly rid his system of Model A's incorrect Say's Law by allowing the aggregate demand and supply of commodities in his system to diverge. Hence Keynes rid his system of the problem of Model A being restricted to long-run states by the system's incorrect Say's Law.

Keynes, however, also rid his system of the key property of Model A's incorrect Say's Law we have described. This is the property that accounts for this incorrect Say's Law providing the basis in Model A for a budget constraint of relevance to microeconomics.

Hence Keynes simultaneously rid his system of the property of Model A's incorrect Say's Law that restricts this system to long-run states as well as of the property of this incorrect Say's Law of providing the basis in Model A for a budget constraint of relevance to microeconomics.

Consequently, the Keynesian system is not restricted to long-run states by Model A's incorrect Say's Law. However, the microeconomics of the real part of the Keynesian system is suppressed. Let us contrast this with Model B'.

To review, we rid Model B' *only* of the property of Model A's incorrect Say's Law that restricts the latter system to long-run states. Hence we did not rid Model B' of the property of Model A's incorrect Say's Law that provides the basis in the system for a budget constraint of relevance to microeconomics.

Instead, we brought this property of Model A's incorrect Say's Law correctly into Model B'. This was by our bringing it into Model B' through the behavior in the system rather than through Say's Law as is the case with Model A.

Hence we preserve in Model B' in a correct manner, the key role of Model A's incorrect Say's Law of providing the basis for a budget constraint of relevance to microeconomics.

9.11 Further Remarks On Why The Microeconomics Of The Real Part Of The Keynesian System Is Suppressed

This book emphasizes that price systems are all necessarily subject to limitation in resources and hence they are all necessarily subject to budget constraints. Next, Model A is characterized by an external budget constraint form of Say's Law that restricts the system to long-run states.

Moreover, both Model B and the Keynesian system are rid of Model A's external budget constraint. However, price systems are all necessarily subject to a budget constraint.

Hence we must ensure that both Model B and the Keynesian system remain characterized by budget constraints. Let us discuss how this was accomplished in Model B then we shall consider the Keynesian system.

On account of the new aspect to behavior that we brought into Model B, we transformed Model A's external budget constraint into an internal budget constraint in Model B. This is a budget constraint which, in being determined within Model B, cannot possibly restrict the system to long-run states.

This is also a budget constraint of relevance to microeconomics in that individual quantities of commodities demanded (supplied) emerge from it. This accounts for Model B being wholly microeconomic in character. Let us now consider the Keynesian system.

Keynes removed from his system Model A's external budget constraint that restricts this latter system to long-run states; and again, since price systems are all necessarily subject to a budget constraint, we must ensure that the Keynesian system remains characterized by a budget constraint. Let us discuss how this is accomplished in the Keynesian system.

Keynes' aggregate demand and supply functions determine the variable W that reflects the system's limited flow of resources. Now the Keynesian system is not commonly looked on as being characterized by an explicit budget constraint.

However, since W reflects the Keynesian system's limited flow of resources, and budget constraints arise from limitation in resources, this implies that W forms the basis for a budget constraint in the Keynesian system.

Moreover, this is an internal budget constraint since it stems from the variable W that is determined internally in the system by Keynes' aggregate demand and supply functions. Hence this Keynesian internal budget constraint cannot possibly restrict the system to long-run states.

However, since this internal budget constraint stems from Keynes' aggregate demand and supply functions, it is clearly not a budget constraint of relevance to microeconomics. This is because individual quantities of commodities demanded (supplied) cannot possibly emerge from it to enter the system's markets.

Instead, the variable W rather than individual quantities of commodities emerge from this internal budget constraint and enters the markets of the Keynesian system. There it is determined by aggregative or macroeconomic market processes. This accounts for the microeconomics of the real part of the Keynesian system being suppressed.

Hence to summarize our analysis, all price systems are necessarily subject to budget constraints. Next, Model B and the Keynesian system are both rid of Model A's external budget constraint that restricts the latter system to long-run states.

However, the new aspect to behavior of Model B accounts for Model A's external budget constraint being transformed into an internal budget constraint in Model B.

This is a budget constraint of relevance to microeconomics; since individual quantities of commodities demanded (supplied) emerge from it. This accounts for Model B being wholly microeconomic in character.

Next, the Keynesian system is also rid of Model A's external budget constraint; and as we discussed, it is implied in Keynesian analysis that this is replaced in the Keynesian system with an internal budget constraint.

This internal budget constraint cannot possibly restrict the system to any specific state. However, the Keynesian system is not characterized by the new aspect to behavior that we brought into Model B.

This means that the internal budget constraint implied in the Keynesian system is not of relevance to microeconomics but only to macroeconomics. This accounts for the microeconomics of the real part of the Keynesian system being suppressed.

This analysis brings out the significance for our new approach to price systems of the new aspect to behavior described in Chapter 1.4 that we brought into our new systems, systems we represent by Model B.

We have discussed how Model B and the Keynesian system are both rid of Model A's incorrect form of Say's Law that restricts the latter system to long-run states.

This is an incorrect form of the Law in that it is not a true identity; since it is a budget constraint that is imposed on Model A to ensure consistency of the system.

Next, Model B and the Keynesian system are both rid of this external budget constraint of Model A. This is by this external budget constraint of Model A being transformed in both

Model B and the Keynesian system into internal budget constraints.

These budget constraints, in being determined internally in Model B and the Keynesian system, cannot possibly restrict these systems to long-run states. However, there is a key difference between Model B and the Keynesian system.

This is because Model B is characterized by the new aspect to behavior described in Chapter1.4 whereas this aspect to behavior is missing from the Keynesian system.

This new aspect to behavior accounts for Model B's internal budget constraint being of relevance to microeconomics; since individual quantities of commodities demanded (supplied) emerge from it. This accounts for Model B being wholly microeconomic in character.

On the other hand, this new aspect to behavior is missing from the Keynesian system. This means that the Keynesian system's internal budget constraint is not of relevance to microeconomics since individual quantities of commodities demanded (supplied) do not emerge from it.

Instead, the overall output or income variable W of the Keynesian system emerges from the system's internal budget constraint and enters the markets of the Keynesian system where it is determined by aggregative or macroeconomic market processes. This accounts for the microeconomics of the real part of the Keynesian system being suppressed.

9.12 The Budget Constraints of Price Systems

Clearly, a key facet to this book lies in our dealing in a more satisfactory manner with the budget constraints of price systems compared to the orthodox approach.

Budget constraints are imposed on orthodox microeconomic price systems such as Model A. These external budget constraints impose a limited flow of resources on the systems hence they restrict the generality of the systems.

This is reflected, for example, in Model A's external budget constraint restricting the system to long-run states. However, we adopted a more general approach to the budget constraints of our new systems.

This approach is reflected in us dealing with the budget constraints of our new systems by dealing with the systems' limited flows of resources that give rise to these budget constraints.

This approach led to the budget constraints of our new systems, systems we represent by Model B, being determined internally in the systems. These internal budget constraints are more general than the externally-imposed budget constraints of orthodox systems such as Model A.

This is because in being determined internally in our new systems, they cannot possibly restrict the systems to any specific states. Through following this approach, we integrated an internal budget constraint into Model B that cannot possibly restrict this system to long-run states.

Moreover, this internal budget constraint accounts for Model B being wholly microeconomic in character since individual quantities of commodities emerge from it. Model A, however, does not reflect this approach to budget constraints which results in this system being characterized by an externally-imposed budget constraint.

However, this external budget constraint while accounting for Model A being wholly microeconomic in character, restricts the system to long-run states. Let us now consider the Keynesian system.

As we discussed in the previous section, the Keynesian system is not commonly looked on as being characterized by an explicit budget constraint. Yet it is implied in Keynesian analysis that the Keynesian system is subject to a budget constraint. This is an internal budget constraint that cannot possibly restrict the system to long-run states.

However, we also discussed how this internal budget constraint of the Keynesian system is of relevance only to macroeconomics. This accounts for this Keynesian budget constraint suppressing the microeconomics of the real part of the Keynesian system.

9.13 Keynes Dealt Only With A Symptom Of The Inconsistency Of Model A

We discussed in Chapter 8.7 how Keynes rid his system of a symptom of the underlying inconsistency of Model A rather than of this inconsistency itself.

This symptom of the inconsistency of Model A is the restriction of the system to long-run states by Say's Law. However, drawing on the analysis of the preceding section we can now go further into this analysis.

To review, the inconsistency of Model A results from consistency of the system with limitation in resources being ensured as a result of Say's Law being imposed on the system rather than by the behavior in the system. We then resolved this inconsistency by bringing the new aspect to behavior described in Chapter 1.4 into Model B.

Now in dealing with the issue of consistency of price systems with limitation in resources, we necessarily also deal with the budget constraints of the systems. This means that since consistency with limitation in resources is not ensured in a satisfactory manner in Model A, the system is also subject to an unsatisfactory budget constraint.

This is reflected in Model A being subject to an external budget constraint that restricts the system to long-run states. Hence in bringing the new aspect to behavior described in Chapter 1.4 into Model B we not only rid this system of the inconsistency of Model A.

We also rid Model B of Model A's external budget constraint that restricts the latter system to long-run states. This was accomplished through the new aspect to behavior of Model B transforming Model A's external budget constraint into an internal budget constraint in Model B. This is a budget constraint that cannot possibly restrict the latter system to long-run states.

Now we have discussed how Keynes also rid his system of Model A's external budget constraint by transforming it into an internal budget constraint; and this Keynesian internal budget constraint cannot possibly restrict the system to long-run states.

Hence we arrive at a similar conclusion through Model B and the Keynesian system which is that both systems are rid of Model A's external budget constraint that restricts the latter system to long-run states.

Moreover, this is accomplished through Model A's external budget constraint being transformed into an internal budget constraint in both Model B and the Keynesian system. However, as we discussed, we accomplish this by our resolving the inconsistency of Model A through Model B.

This was by bringing the new aspect to behavior described in Chapter 1.4 into the latter system. That is, we accomplish this through microeconomics. This accounts for Model B being wholly microeconomic in character.

Keynes, however, bypassed this whole process we have described whereby we rid Model B of Model A's external budget constraint by transforming it into an internal budget constraint in Model B. Yet Keynes also rid his system of Model A's external budget constraint by transforming it into an internal budget constraint in his system.

This, however, was accomplished through Keynes' use of macroeconomics. This reflects how Keynes resolved a symptom of the inconsistency of Model A rather than this inconsistency itself.

This symptom is the restriction of Model A to long-run states by the system's incorrect form of Say's Law. But Keynes' approach accounts for the microeconomics of the real part of his system being suppressed.

This is because to resolve the inconsistency of Model A rather than a symptom of this inconsistency, we had to bring the new aspect to behavior described in Chapter 1.4 into Model B. This required the use of microeconomics in the latter system; and this accounts for Model B being wholly microeconomic in character.

9.14 Summary

Keynes held that Model A is restricted to long-run states by Say's Law. However, we established that while Model A is restricted to long-run states, this is because of an incorrect or misused form of Say's Law that characterizes the system.

This incorrect form of the Law enters Model A because of the inconsistency we uncovered in the system. Hence to resolve the problem of Model A being restricted to long-run states, we need to rid the system of this inconsistency.

This was accomplished through Model B, this system hence being rid of Model A's incorrect form of Say's Law. This moreover was accomplished in a manner which ensured that Model B is wholly microeconomic in character.

Keynes also rid his system of Model A's incorrect form of Say's Law. This, however, was accomplished in a manner that accounts that for the microeconomics of the real part of the Keynesian system being suppressed.

Clearly, a key part of the chapter lies in our bringing out how it is because the Keynesian system lacks the new aspect to behavior of Model B that accounts for Keynes ridding his system of Model A's incorrect Say's Law in an unsatisfactory manner.

To review, Model A's incorrect Say's Law has the following two properties. First, this incorrect Say's Law accounts for the system being restricted to long-run states. Second, this incorrect Say's Law yet provides the basis in Model A for a budget constraint of relevance to microeconomics.

Now Keynes allowed the aggregate demand and supply of commodities in his system to diverge to wholly rid his system of Model A's incorrect Say's Law. This rid the Keynesian system of both of the properties of Model A's incorrect Say's Law that we described.

This means that the Keynesian system, in being rid of the first property of Model A's incorrect Say's Law, is not restricted to long-run states by Model A's incorrect Say's Law. However, the Keynesian system is also rid of the second property of Model A's incorrect Say's Law.

This, to review, is the property that accounts for this incorrect Say's Law providing the basis in Model A for a budget constraint that is of relevance to microeconomics in that individual quantities of commodities emerge from it.

Keynes' ridding his system of this second property of Model A's incorrect Say's Law accounts for the microeconomics of the real part of his system being suppressed.

In contrast, on account of the new aspect to behavior that we brought into Model B, we rid this system *only* of the property of Model A's incorrect Say's Law that restricts this system to long-run states.

Hence we retain in Model B through the system's correct Say's Law, the property of Model A's incorrect Say's Law of providing the basis in Model A for a budget constraint of relevance to microeconomics.

This was by our bringing this property correctly into Model B by bringing it into the system through the behavior in the system. This accounted for Model B being wholly microeconomic in character

On the other hand, this property is brought incorrectly into Model A since it is brought into the system by Say's Law. This is on account of Say's Law being imposed on the system to eliminate a surplus equation to ensure that the system is consistent.

We also confirmed in Section 9.11 from another perspective that the microeconomics of the real part of the Keynesian system is suppressed. To review, the Keynesian system is not commonly looked on as being characterized by an explicit budget constraint.

However, it is implied in Keynesian analysis that the Keynesian system reflects an internal budget constraint that cannot possibly restrict the system to any specific state. But this is a budget constraint that is of relevance only to macroeconomics since individual quantities of commodities do not emerge from it.

Instead, the macroeconomic variable W emerges from the Keynesian system's internal budget constraint and enters the system's market processes. This accounts for the microeconomics of the real part of the Keynesian system being suppressed. This is the part of the system that deals with aggregate demand and supply variables.

Chapter 10

Market Processes In The Revised Classical System

10.1 Introduction

We have established that we have rid Model B of an incorrect form of Say's Law that characterizes Model A and which restricts this latter system to long-run states. This was by our first establishing that Model A's incorrect Say's Law is an external budget constraint that accounts for the system being restricted to long-run states.

However, we rid Model B of this external budget constraint of Model A by transforming it into an internal budget constraint in Model B. This is a budget constraint which as we discussed in Chapters 2.7 and 6.3 is a true identity that cannot possibly restrict Model B to long-run states.

Next, we discussed in Chapter 7 how Model A is characterized by long-run market processes that stem from the system's incorrect Say's Law. This imbeds non-behavioral long-run market processes into Model A that restrict the system to long-run states.

However, we also established in Chapter 7 that Model B is consistent with the existence of behavioral long-run market processes; and we shall establish in this chapter that such processes exist in the system. This will be accomplished through a monetary form of Model B.

Through this monetary form of Model B we shall resolve the problems of the price level indeterminacy and invalid real-monetary dichotomy of Model A. These are problems that were raised by Patinkin and which we discussed in Chapter 3.8.

We shall also review in this chapter all of the systems that are set out in this book. This will show that through our new systems, we successively revised the orthodox classical system, Model A, to give it a more general character.

Finally, this chapter deals explicitly with how prices in our systems move to equilibrium. Hence since we are dealing with classical-neoclassical analysis, we need to follow the classical-neoclassical literature and assume a *tâtonnement* and recontract process when discussing how prices move to equilibrium in the systems.

10.2 A Monetary Form Of The Revised Classical System

We discussed in Chapter 3.8 how Model A, the orthodox classical system, is usually complemented with the Cambridge cash balance equation in order to determine the system's price level.

We shall in order to put our analysis on a par with the literature, initially follow a similar approach reflected in our complementing Model B, the real form of our revised classical system, with the Cambridge cash balance equation. Below is the Cambridge cash balance equation:

8. $\quad K\big[p_1 X_1 + p_2 X_2 + \cdots p_n X_n\big] = M$

We discussed in Chapter 3.8 how the variable K represents the proportion of their money income that individuals and firms hold as a cash balance; and we again assume that these balances are held only for transactions purposes. That is, to offset any possible lack of synchronization between payments and receipts.

Next, overall money income in Model A is represented by the term $\big[p_1 X_1 + p_2 X_2 + \cdots p_n X_n\big]$ in (8) where $X_1, X_2, ..., X_n$ are the equilibrium quantities of commodities each of which is multiplied by the appropriate price.

Hence the whole expression to the left of the equality sign in (8) is the demand for money to hold for transactions purposes. While M, to the right of (8), is the given supply of nominal money. We next show Model B below. This is less detailed form of our revised classical system that is best suited for the present analyses:

Model B

11. $\quad D_j \equiv F_j'\big[f(z)\big]$

12. $\quad S_j \equiv G_j'\big[g(z)\big]$

13. $\quad E_j'\big[f(z) - g(z) = 0\big] = 0$

Let us assume that Model B is in general equilibrium hence we can solve for the system's equilibrium quantities and relative prices. Then we substitute these equilibrium quantities and relative prices from Model B into equation (8) which is the Cambridge constraint.

This allows us to solve for the individual money prices or the price level from equation (8). This leads to Model C which reflects Model B when this system is complemented with the Cambridge cash balance equation.

10.3 Resolving The Price Level Indeterminacy Of Model A Through Model C

Model B, our revised classical system, appears below:

Model B

11. $\quad D_j \equiv F'_j[f(z)]$

12. $\quad S_j \equiv G'_j[g(z)]$

13. $\quad E'_j[f(z)-g(z)=0]=0$

Next, the Cambridge cash balance equation also appears below:

8. $\quad K[p_1 X_1 + p_2 X_2 + \cdots p_n X_n] = M$

Let us now hold the relative commodity prices fixed throughout Model B and move the price level in expression (8), which we shall refer to as P, from equilibrium.

This is through making an equiproportionate change in every individual money price in (8). This throws equation (8) out of equilibrium to hence show some excess demand (supply) of money to hold.

Next, by Walras Law this should result in an equal excess supply (demand) for commodities; and Model B's commodity markets in the aggregate do come out of equilibrium to show this equal excess supply (demand) for commodities. Hence a market process is set up to move P back to equilibrium, Model C's price level hence being determinate.

We need, however, to establish why Model C's commodity markets in the aggregate can come out of equilibrium when the price level is moved from equilibrium; since this is a key property of Model C that distinguishes this system from Model A.

Now the real part of Model C which is Model B, determines $(n-1)$ *relative* commodity demands (supplies) as functions of the relative prices. This explains why when there is an excess demand (supply) of money, Model C's budget constraint,

162

which is Walras Law, shows that there is an equal excess supply (demand) for commodities.

This is because the existence of this overall excess supply (demand) for commodities in Model C is perfectly consistent with the *relative* commodity demands (supplies) that are determined in the real part of the system, that is, in Model B.

Consequently, there are market forces in Model C to move the system back to equilibrium since Walras Law holds when the system is out of equilibrium.

Yet Model C is a dichotomized system because we solve for the relative commodity prices, the z, from conditions $f(z)-g(z)=0$ of Model B without specifying the price level. Clearly, however, this is a valid dichotomy since it does not cause the system's price level to be indeterminate.

Model A is also characterized by a dichotomy since we also solve for the relative prices in the system without specifying the price level. However, Model A's dichotomy as Patinkin emphasized is invalid since it accounts for the system's price level being indeterminate.

10.4 Why Model A's Price Level Indeterminacy Could Be Resolved Through Model C

Let us first discuss in general how a dichotomy between absolute and relative prices is brought into a system. This requires that a subset of equilibrium conditions exist in the system that solve for the equilibrium values of relative prices without the solution for these relative prices being in any way dependent on the absolute level of prices.

Let us now consider Model A in the context of the preceding remarks. This system appears below:

Model A

4. $\quad D_j \equiv F_j\left[z\right]$

5. $\quad S_j \equiv G_j\left[z\right]$

6. $\quad E_j\left[z\right]=0$

We solve for the relative prices, the z, from equation (6) independently of the system's price level. This equation stems from functions (4) and (5) that make absolute commodity demands and supplies depend only on the relative prices.

Hence these absolute commodity demands (supplies) are determined independently of the monetary sector. This explains why Model A's price level which we denote by P is indeterminate; since were the price level moved from equilibrium, the commodity markets remain in equilibrium.

This is because absolute commodity demands (supplies) depend on the relative prices which remain unchanged when the price level is moved from equilibrium. Hence no market equilibrating process is set up to move P back to equilibrium with P hence being indeterminate.

Clearly, Model A's price level is indeterminate because absolute quantities of commodities demanded (supplied) are determined independently of the monetary sector.

This, to review, is because these absolute commodity demands (supplies), in depending only on the relative prices remain unchanged when the price level is moved from equilibrium. Hence no market equilibrating process is set up to move P back to equilibrium with P hence being indeterminate.

However, only relative commodity demands and relative commodity supplies can be determined independently of the monetary sector of the classical system. Let us go into this in detail through focusing on Model B, our revised classical system, which appears below:

Model B

11. $D_j \equiv F_j'[f(z)]$

12. $S_j \equiv G_j'[g(z)]$

13. $E_j'[f(z)-g(z)=0]=0$

We solve for Model B's relative prices, the z, from conditions $f(z)-g(z)=0$ independently of the system's price level. These conditions stem from functions (11) and (12) that make relative commodity demands (supplies) depend on the relative prices, the z.

Consequently, it is these *relative* commodity demands (supplies) and hence the subset of conditions $f(z)-g(z)=0$ that are independent of the monetary sector of Model B. This accounts for us resolving through Model C the price level indeterminacy of Model A along the lines discussed in the previous section.

Clearly, the key difference between Model A and Model B is as follows: the real sector of Model B determines only $(n-1)$ *relative* commodity demands (supplies).

On the other hand, the real sector of Model A determines *absolute* commodity demands (supplies) for all n commodities. Consequently, Walras Law can operate in Model B when the system is out of equilibrium but not in Model A.

10.5 Further Remarks On Resolving Model A's Price Level Indeterminacy And Invalid Dichotomy

We show Model B, our revised classical system again below:

Model B

11. $\quad D_j \equiv F'_j[f(z)]$

12. $\quad S_j \equiv G'_j[g(z)]$

13. $\quad E'_j[f(z) - g(z) = 0] = 0$

We brought the new aspect to behavior described in Chapter 1.4 into Model B through functions $f(z)$ and $g(z)$; and it is through these functions, and hence through this new aspect to behavior, that we have rid Model B of Model A's price level indeterminacy and invalid dichotomy. This may also be established in the following way.

Had we not resolved Model A's inconsistency through Model B, the microeconomic conditions of this latter system, namely, conditions $f(z) - g(z) = 0$ in (13) would have to be replaced by those of the orthodox Model A that were set out in Chapter 3.4.

That is, by the latter system's excess-demand equations, that is, equations $E_j[z] = 0$ of Model A. These orthodox conditions, however, would conflict with the Cambridge equation that characterizes Model C.

This latter system would then be transformed into Model A and an orthodox quantity theory of money equation which as Lange and Patinkin have shown, cannot be integrated in a satisfactory manner.

However, in ridding Model A of inconsistency through Model B, we replaced the set of orthodox microeconomic conditions $E_j[z] = 0$ of Model A with the set of microeconomic conditions $f(z) - g(z) = 0$ in (13) of Model B.

These microeconomic conditions of Model B bring consistency between the real and monetary parts of Model C, the monetary form of Model B. This accounted for us resolving through Model C, the price level indeterminacy and invalid real-monetary dichotomy of Model A.

Finally, Lange prior to Patinkin had brought out a contradiction in Model A which Lange took as a classical system. Lange formed Model A by imposing Say's Law on the system then he deduced the "homogeneity postulate" from the Law.

Next, Lange held that Say's Law is imposed on Model A in order to ensure money neutrality but the Law accounts for the system's price level being indeterminate. This led Lange to conclude that there is a contradiction in Model A.[17]

This is because if the system's price level is to be made determinate, money neutrality must be abandoned through Say's Law being removed from the system. However, this contradiction in Model A that Lange pointed to has also been resolved through Model B.

This is because money is neutral in Model B since we solve for the system's relative prices independently of the price level. As well, the system's price level is determinate as we have established through Model C, the monetary form of Model B. This reflects how we rid the latter system of the contradiction in Model A that Lange brought out.

10.6 An Integrated Monetary Form Of Model C

We have discussed how functions $f(z)$ and $g(z)$ of Model B in determining relative commodity demands (supplies), allowed us as we discussed in Sections 10.3 and 10.4 to impose the Cambridge equation in a consistent manner on Model B to form Model C.

This accounted for us resolving through Model C, the problems of the price level indeterminacy and invalid dichotomy of Model A.

This implies that we may bring the Cambridge equation directly into the general equilibrium equations of Model B rather than following the orthodox complementing procedure that we have used in forming Model C.

Hence we shall now integrate the Cambridge money equation directly into the general equilibrium equations of

---

[17] O. Lange, "Say's Law: A Restatement and Criticism," in *Studies in Mathematical Economics and Econometrics* (Chicago, *1942*), pps. 49-68.

Model B. This will lead to what we shall refer to as an integrated monetary form of Model C to be called Model C'.

Model C' is a system in which the Cambridge long-run money equation is integrated directly into the general equilibrium equations of Model B rather than being added to the system through the orthodox complementary procedure that we have discussed.

Let us proceed with these analyses by drawing on Model B, the real form of our revised classical system, which appears below:

Model B

11. $\quad D_j \equiv F'_j[f(z)]$

12. $\quad S_j \equiv G'_j[g(z)]$

13. $\quad E'_j[f(z)-g(z)=0]=0$

Model B's demand and supply functions are real long-run relative demand and supply functions since the system deals only with commodities which exclude money. Hence the interior functions $f(z)$ and $g(z)$ on which they are based are real interior functions.

On the other hand, the demand and supply functions of Model C' are monetary long-run relative demand and supply functions; and these will be based on monetary interior functions. These monetary interior functions appear below:

14. $\quad R_1 \equiv f_1(K)$

15. $\quad S_1 \equiv g_1(P)$

Let us refer to the variable R_1 in expression (14). This variable is the ratio of the quantity of money demanded for transactions purposes to the overall quantity of commodities demanded, the latter being measured in money.

This ratio is made a function of the Cambridge K as shown in (14). This latter variable is taken from the Cambridge cash-balance version of the long-run quantity theory of money that was introduced in Chapter 3.8.

Next, the variable S_1 in (15) is the ratio of the fixed money supply to the overall quantity of commodities supplied, the latter also being measured in money. This ratio depends on the price level, P, as shown in (15) since both the money supply and the overall supply of commodities in real terms are now held fixed.

Clearly, the monetary interior functions of Model C' are consistent with Walras Law. Moreover, these monetary interior functions put the Cambridge cash-balance equation in a form that brings out how this equation has a relative character like Model B.

This, in fact, is what allows us to integrate the Cambridge equation directly into the general equilibrium conditions of Model B to form Model C'. This system which we refer to an integrated monetary form of Model C appears below:

Model C'

16. $\quad D_j \equiv F_j''[f_1(K), f(z)]$

17. $\quad S_j \equiv G_j''[g_1(P), g(z)]$

18. $\quad E_j''[f_1(K)-g_1(P) = 0, f(z)-g(z)=0] = 0$

We arrived at the demand and supply functions of Model C', functions (16) and (17), by substituting the monetary interior functions, functions (14) and (15), into the demand and supply functions (11) and (12) of Model B. These lead to equations (18), the system's excess-demand equations.

10.7 Consistency Of The Monetary Model C'

We show the monetary Model C' again below:

Model C'

16. $\quad D_j \equiv F_j''[f_1(K), f(z)]$

17. $\quad S_j \equiv G_j''[g_1(P), g(z)]$

18. $\quad E_j''[f_1(K)-g_1(P) = 0, f(z)-g(z)=0] = 0$

Model C' must be interpreted in the same way in which we interpreted the real Model B. That is, the overall excess-demand equations $E_j''[\,]=0$ in (18) determine the market behavior of the system in determining the excess-demands that enter the system's markets.

However, the overall equations $E_j''[\,]=0$ themselves, and hence the market behavior of the system depends on or is constrained by the elements that are internal to these overall functions. These internal elements, in turn, stem from our new approach to the behavior of individuals and firms.

This behavior as will now be discussed, ensures that Model C' is automatically consistent. Let us assume that the overall conditions $E_j''[\,]=0$ in (18) vanish, the system hence being in general equilibrium.

This is only possible were both internal conditions within conditions $E_j''[\,]=0$ to vanish. We next assume that the monetary condition, namely, condition $f_1(K)-g_1(P)=0$ first vanishes. This allows us to solve for the price level, P of Model C'.

There are now the real conditions meaning conditions $f(z)-g(z)=0$ remaining within (18); and the vanishing of these conditions, which are $(n-1)$ in number, determines the $(n-1)$ relative prices, the z.

Moreover, the vanishing of these latter conditions causes the overall conditions $E_j''[\,]=0$ in (18) to now vanish, the system hence being in general equilibrium. This means that P and the z are determined in general equilibrium. As well, they are determined independently of each other, reflecting how money is neutral in the system.

Consequently, the integrated monetary Model C' is automatically consistent as was also the case with the real Model B. Model C' allows us to readily illustrate the greater generality of this system compared to Model A. Model C' appears again bellow:

Model C'

16. $\quad D_j \equiv F_j''[f_1(K), f(z)]$
17. $\quad S_j \equiv G_j''[g_1(P), g(z)]$
18. $\quad E_j''[f_1(K)-g_1(P)=0, f(z)-g(z)=0]=0$

Let us hold the relative prices fixed throughout the system move the price level P in the monetary condition $f_1(K)-g_1(P)=0$ (18) from equilibrium. This leads to an excess demand (supply) of money that is matched by an equal excess demand (supply) of commodities.

This sets up a market process that moves P back to equilibrium. Hence the price level of Model C' is determinate. This, however, is only possible because there is consistency between the real and monetary parts of the system.

As discussed, when P in the monetary part of Model C' namely $f_1(K)-g_1(P)=0$ in (18) is moved from equilibrium, a market mechanism is set up to move P back to equilibrium.

This process, however, can only exist because of the set of real conditions namely, conditions $f(z)-g(z)=0$ that are also within (18). This is because these conditions as we have established earlier allow this market mechanism to exist. Let us now consider Model A.

We replaced the latter system's microeconomic conditions $E_j[z]=0$ with the microeconomic conditions $f(z)-g(z)=0$. Were this not done, Model A's microeconomic conditions $E_j[z]=0$ would conflict with the monetary condition $f_1(K)-g_1(P)=0$ in (18) of Model C'.

This system would thereby be transformed into Model A and the Cambridge cash balance equation which, as Lange and Patinkin have shown, cannot be integrated in a satisfactory manner. This accounts for Model A being characterized by an indeterminate price level and invalid dichotomy, problems now resolved through Model C'.

10.8 Review Of The Orthodox And New Systems

We shall now review all of the systems that were set out in this book. Model A', the preliminary form of Model A that was formed in Chapter 3.3 appears below:

Model A'

1. $D_j \equiv F(p_j)$
2. $S_j \equiv G(p_j)$
3. $E(p_j)=0$

We then imposed the orthodox "homogeneity postulate" on Model A' to make the system's commodity demands and supplies depend on the relative rather than on the absolute prices to rid the system of "money illusion."

We thereby transformed Model A' into Model A, the orthodox classical system which appears below. We pointed out earlier that Model A was developed in neoclassical analysis and is hence frequently referred to as a neoclassical system.

However, Model A is also widely taken as a formal version of the classical system which is the approach we follow in this book.

Model A

4. $D_j \equiv F_j[z]$

5. $S_j \equiv G_j[z]$

6. $E_j[z] = 0$

Next, we formed Model B below, our revised classical system by bringing functions $f(z)$ and $g(z)$ and hence the new aspect to behavior described in Chapter 1.4 into Model A.

Model B

11. $D_j \equiv F'_j[f(z)]$

12. $S_j \equiv G'_j[g(z)]$

13. $E'_j[f(z) - g(z) = 0] = 0$

We then set out in this chapter a monetary form of Model B, namely, Model C. We arrived at Model C by complementing Model B with the Cambridge money equation. Then through Model C we resolved the price level indeterminacy and invalid real-monetary dichotomy of Model A as discussed in Sections 10.3 and 10.4.

Next, we integrated the Cambridge cash balance equation directly into the general equilibrium equations of Model B to form Model C' below.

Model C'

16. $D_j \equiv F'''_j[f_1(K), f(z)]$

17. $S_j \equiv G'''_j[g_1(P), g(z)]$

18. $E'''_j[f_1(K) - g_1(P) = 0, f(z) - g(z) = 0] = 0$

We could integrate the Cambridge equation directly into Model B to form Model C' because we first brought out through functions (14) and (15) how the Cambridge equation has a relative character like Model B.

This explained why the Cambridge equation, through functions ((14) and (15), could be directly integrated into Model B to form Model C'.

We referred to Model C' as an integrated monetary form of Model C; and we may also as we did through Model C, establish that Model C' is rid of the price level indeterminacy and invalid real-monetary dichotomy that characterize Model A.

Consequently, through our new systems we successively revised the orthodox classical system Model A to put it into a more general form as finally reflected in Model C'.

10.9 Summary

We have rid Model B of an incorrect form of Say's Law that characterizes Model A and which restricts this latter system to long-run states.

This was by our first establishing that Model A's incorrect Say's Law is an external budget constraint that accounts for the system being restricted to long-run states. This explains why this external budget constraint is not a true identity form of Say's Law.

However, we rid Model B of this external budget constraint of Model A by transforming it into an internal budget constraint in Model B. This is a budget constraint that cannot possibly restrict Model B to long-run states. This explains why this internal budget constraint is a true identity form of Say's Law.

Next, Model A as discussed in Chapter 7 is characterized by long-run market processes that stem from the system's incorrect Say's Law. This imbeds non-behavioral long-run market processes into Model A that restrict the system to long-run states.

However, we also established in Chapter 7 that Model B is consistent with the existence of behavioral long-run market processes; and we established in this chapter that such processes exist in the system.

This was accomplished in Sections 10.3 and 10.4 through a monetary form of Model B namely Model C. This was through our establishing that Model C is rid of the price level indeterminacy and invalid real-monetary dichotomy of Model A.

We then put Model C into the form of Model C' which we referred to as an integrated form of Model C. Hence we may also establish that Model C' like Model C is rid of the price level indeterminacy and invalid dichotomy of Model A.

We also discussed how Model B is a dichotomized system in that we can solve for the system's relative prices without specifying the price level. However, Model B's dichotomy is not invalid like Model A's dichotomy.

This is because Model B's dichotomy does not cause the system's price level to be indeterminate. On the other hand, Model A's dichotomy as Patinkin established causes this system's price level to be indeterminate. This explains why Model A's dichotomy is invalid.

Clearly, a key part of the chapter lay is how we established consistency between the real and monetary parts of Model B; since this allowed us through this system to resolve the price level indeterminacy and invalid dichotomy of Model A.

To review, the following requirement is needed to bring a dichotomy between absolute and relative prices into a system.

This is that there be a subset of equilibrium conditions in the system that solve for the equilibrium values of relative prices without the solution for the relative prices being in any way dependent on the absolute level of prices.

Next, such a subset of equilibrium conditions exists in both Model A and Model B. These, however, determine absolute commodity demands (supplies) in Model A as functions of the relative prices. This as Patinkin has established accounts for Model A's price level indeterminacy and invalid dichotomy.

However, only *relative* commodity demands and *relative* commodity supplies can be determined independently of the classical system's monetary sector; and Model B, our revised classical system, has a subset of equilibrium conditions that determine such relative commodity demands (supplies) as functions of the relative prices.

This brought consistency between the real and monetary parts of Model B. This then allowed us to establish through Model C, the monetary form of Model B, that we resolved the price level indeterminacy and invalid real-monetary dichotomy of Model A, the orthodox classical system.

Clearly, the key difference between Model A and Model B is as follows: the real sector of Model B determines only $(n-1)$ *relative* commodity demands (supplies).

On the other hand, the real sector of Model A determines *absolute* commodity demands (supplies) for all n commodities. Consequently, Walras Law can operate in Model B when the system is out of equilibrium but not in Model A.

Finally, we reviewed all of the systems that were set out in this book. This showed that through our new systems, we successively revised the orthodox classical system,

Model A, to give it a more general character as finally reflected in Model C'.

Chapter 11

Issues Concerning Consistency Of The Classical System

11.1 Introduction

There is a basic theme running through this book which is that our revised classical system, Model B, is based wholly on economic principles or economic behavior. This is in the sense that there is no interference with these principles or behavior in Model B stemming from non-behavioral elements such as Say's Law.

On the other hand, the behavior or economic rationale of the orthodox classical system, Model A, is restricted by the non-behavioral Say's Law which limits the generality of the system.

We shall proceed by first discussing how we may look on the inconsistency of Model A as causing a gap in the system's behavioral content. This will assist us in bringing out how Say's Law is misused in Model A.

This is because the *non-behavioral Law* is brought into the picture to fill the gap in the system's *behavioral content*. We shall also review aspects of the controversies that arose in response to Patinkin's claim that Model A is inconsistent in an economic sense.

11.2 There Is A Gap In The Behavioral Content Of Model A

All price systems are characterized by a general logic this being reflected in the systems being consistent with limitation in resources.

That is, in the quantities of commodities demanded and supplied each summing to the systems' limited resources to hence exhaust these resources. Two conditions are required to bring this logic into a system.

First, there must be an explicit variable in the system that reflects the system's limited resources. Second, the commodity demands and supplies determined in the system must sum to these limited resources. These are the two conditions that are required to capture a system's general logic.

In this book we raise the issue of how these two conditions are brought into a system in order to capture the general logic of the system; and it is through our exploring this issue that we uncovered, and ultimately resolved, the economic inconsistency of Model A. Let us first focus on Model B then we shall consider Model Λ.

We set out in Chapter 1.4 the new aspect to behavior that we bring into Model B; and in Chapter 1.6 we derived the variable W that reflects Model B's limited flow of resources.

Now the new aspect behavior that we brought into Model B, to review, is reflected in individuals and firms being aware that their resources are limited. Hence they act light of this awareness by determining quantities of commodities demanded (supplied) that exhaust their limited resources.

That is, there are two aspects to this behavior; and the first one brings Model B's limited flow of resources W into the behavioral content of the system. While the other ensures that Model B's commodity demands and supplies each sum to the system's limited resources W.

These, as we discussed, are the conditions that are required to ensure that Model B reflects consistency with limitation in resources. Hence these conditions are ensured in Model B by the behavior in the system.

That is, consistency of Model B with limitation in resources is ensured by the behavior in the system. As a result, Model B reflects the general *economic* logic that should characterize all price systems. Let us now consider Model A.

This latter system, of course, reflects consistency with limitation in resources in that the quantities of commodities demanded (supplied) each sum to the system's limited flow of resources to exhaust these resources.

However, unlike Model B, the variable W which also reflects the limited flow of resources of Model A is imposed on the system from the outside by Say's Law. This is on account of Say's Law being imposed on Model A to ensure consistency of the system by eliminating a surplus equation from the system.

This ensures that the quantities of commodities demanded (supplied) each sum to Model A's limited flow of resources W. That is, consistency of Model A with limitation in resources is ensured in Model A.

This, however, is ensured by the non-behavioral Say's Law being imposed on the system to eliminate a surplus equation rather than by the behavior in the system. This brings inconsistency into Model A.

176

On the other hand, consistency with limitation in resources is ensured in Model B by the behavior in the system which rids Model B of the inconsistency of Model A. Let us discuss more generally what accounts for this difference between Model A and Model B.

In forming price systems, we need to have in mind from the outset that the systems must all necessarily reflect behavior that is consistent with limitation in resources; and in writing Model B we do ensure this from the outset.

This is by our writing Model B's demand and supply functions in a manner so that they incorporate the new aspect to behavior described in Chapter 1.4. This accounts for consistency of Model B with limitation in resources being ensured by the behavior in the system. Let us now consider Model A.

Economists in writing Model A do not ensure from the outset that this system reflects consistency with limitation in resources. This is because they do not incorporate into this system's demand and supply functions the new aspect to behavior described in Chapter 1.4.

Consequently, there is a gap in the behavioral content of Model A since the aspect to behavior described in Chapter 1.4 is missing from the system. This in turn accounts for Model A being initially inconsistent which is reflected in there being a surplus equation over the number of unknowns.

Economists then impose Say's Law on the system to eliminate this surplus equation to ensure consistency of the system through the system meeting the counting rule; and this ensures that Model A is consistent with limitation in resources.

Hence Say's Law which is non-behavioral in character comes into the picture to fill the gap in the system's *behavioral content*. This is to ensure that the system is consistent with limitation in resources.

This, however, accounts for the inconsistency in Model A; since consistency of the system with limitation in resources should be ensured by the behavior in the system as is the case with Model B.

11.3 Controversies Concerning Consistency Of Model A

We discussed in Chapter 4.5 how Patinkin held that Model A is inconsistent in an economic sense. Moreover, we also discussed how some economists, in contrast, took Model A to be consistent on the basis that the system can be solved for equilibrium. That is, on the basis that the system meets the counting rule.

However, this book shows that taking Model A to be consistent solely on the basis of the system being made by Say's Law consistent is an unsatisfactory approach to ensuring consistency of Model A.

Archibald and Lipsey were among several economists who held that Model A is consistent in that it can be solved for equilibrium. [18] Yet Archibald and Lipsey also recognized, as Patinkin had held, that Model A lacked market equilibrating processes that are needed to determine the system's price level.

Hence Archibald and Lipsey concluded that Patinkin's real-balance approach was indeed useful in bringing market equilibrating processes into the system to move it to equilibrium.

Nonetheless, Archibald and Lipsey's main point was that Model A is consistent in that it can be solved for equilibrium. That is, that the system meets the counting rule. In this way they defended Model A from Patinkin's charge that the system is inconsistent in an economic sense.

However, Archibald and Lipsey left Model A untouched and hence still characterized by the price level indeterminacy and invalid dichotomy brought out by Patinkin. In contrast, these problems were resolved in this book through Model B.

True, Model A is consistent in meeting the counting rule as Archibald and Lipsey emphasized. How this is accomplished through the non-behavioral Say's Law being imposed on the system to eliminate a surplus equation.

This brought inconsistency into Model A; since the system should be made to conform to the counting rule by the behavior in the system. This is the case with Model B.

Hence through the latter system we resolved the inconsistency of Model A; and this also accounted for us resolving through the latter system the problems with Model A raised by Patinkin.

11.4 Inconsistency And Surplus Demand And Supply Functions In Model A.

Model A's demand and supply functions lead to a surplus equation over the number of unknowns; and we showed that this

---

[18] G.C Archibald and R.G. Lipsey, "Monetary and Value Theory: A Critique of Lange and Patinkin", *Review of Economic Studies* (1958), pps. 1-22.

is due to an economic inconsistency. This is because the system's functions, and hence the behavior in the system, does not ensure that the system is consistent with limitation in resources.

This, in turn, leads to Model A being initially inconsistent which is reflected in there being a surplus equation over the number of unknowns. Hence Model A's functions should be revised so that they ensure consistency of the system with limited resources.

Economists instead commonly impose Say's Law on the system to eliminate Model A's surplus equation to make the system consistent by ensuring that it meets the counting rule.

This as we established earlier ensures that the system is consistent with limitation in resources. This means of ensuring consistency of Model A with limitation in resources, however, brings the inconsistency we have uncovered into the system.

This is because consistency of Model A with limitation in resources should be ensured by the behavior or economic rationale of the system rather by Say's Law.

Model A's inconsistency hence had to be resolved by our transforming Model A's functions into the relative demand and supply functions of Model B. These latter functions ensure consistency of Model B with limited resources, to hence resolve through Model B, Model A's economic inconsistency.

These new functions, moreover, automatically ensure equality of the number of independent equations and the number of unknowns in Model B. As a result, there is no need to eliminate a surplus demand and supply function from Model B to make the system consistent. Let us consider Model A.

Model A, of course, is consistent with limitation in resources; but consistency with limited resources is ensured in Model A through an incorrect form of Say's Law being imposed on the system to make the system consistent. This is through the Law eliminating a surplus equation from Model A.

This results in one demand and one supply function being made redundant and hence being eliminated from Model A to make the system consistent by meeting the counting rule.

However, the initial existence of Model A's surplus functions is a result of the system being inconsistent with limited resources. Then the system is made consistent with limited resources but in an incorrect manner.

That is, by an incorrect form of Say's Law being imposed on Model A to make the system meet the counting rule rather than by revision of the system's demand and supply functions;

and this incorrect Say's Law results in one demand and one supply function being made redundant.

Hence the need to eliminate these functions is forced on Model A by the economic inconsistency of this system's demand and supply functions. This is readily confirmed.

When we replaced Model A's functions with the relative demand and supply functions of Model B, these latter functions ensure consistency of Model B with the system's limited resources.

As well, Model B's functions also automatically ensure consistency of the system in leading to equality between the number of independent equations and unknowns. Hence there was now no need to eliminate a surplus demand and a surplus supply function from Model B.

This means that the initial existence of a surplus demand and supply function in Model A is a reflection of the initial economic inconsistency of the system's demand and supply functions.

Furthermore, the elimination of these surplus functions by imposing an incorrect form of Say's Law on Model A to make the system consistent, is a reflection of this inconsistency of Model A being incorrectly resolved.

This is because this inconsistency should be resolved, in the first place, by revision of Model A's demand and supply functions to transform them into Model B's functions. This is the course followed in this book.

This made the whole issue of the existence of a surplus demand and supply function that characterize Model A, and hence the need to eliminate these functions, redundant in the case of Model B.

11.5 Remarks On Consistency Of Price Systems

This book establishes that consistency of a price system as being reflected in equality between the number of the system's independent equations and unknowns should not be imposed on a system.

Instead, consistency should stem from the system's economics and hence from the system's demand and supply functions. This is readily confirmed by referring to Model A and Model B, the orthodox and revised classical systems.

Model A, to review, is initially inconsistent in that there is surplus equation over the number of unknowns. Then the system is made consistent by the counting rule being imposed on the system through Say's Law being used to eliminate the system's surplus equation.

This procedure, however, accounts for Model A being restricted to long-run states by the system's incorrect or misused form of the Law. Let us now consider Model B. We brought the new aspect to behavior described in Chapter 1.4 into the latter system.

This ensured that Model B reflects the general economic logic that should underlie all price systems. Moreover, this new aspect to behavior as discussed in Chapter 6.4 ensures that Model B automatically meets the counting rule.

This meant that we did not need Say's Law to ensure consistency of Model B. Hence Model B is rid of the incorrect form of the Law of Model A that is imposed on the system to make it consistent but which restricts this system to long-run states.

As a result, Model B has a more general character than Model A in that Model B is not restricted to long-run states by an incorrect or misused form of Say's Law as is the case with Model A.

This analysis has basic implications for the counting rule that is imposed on orthodox systems such as Model A to ensure equality between the number of independent equations and the number of unknowns in the systems. This equality must hold in all systems.

However, it must be ensured by consistency of a system's general economic logic as is the case with Model B. True, independent equations and unknowns are equal in Model A. However, this is ensured by the counting rule being imposed on this system.

This is through Say's Law being imposed on the system to eliminate a surplus equation. This brings an incorrect form of Say's Law into Model A that restricts the system to long-run states. This, however, has been resolved through Model B.

This is because as we established in Chapter 6.4, consistency of Model B in the sense of the system meeting the counting rule is ensured by the behavior in the system. Hence we do not need Model A's incorrect Say's Law to ensure that Model B meets the counting rule. This rids Model B of Model A's incorrect Say's Law that restricts the latter system to long-run states.

11.6 Review Of The Implications Of The Book For The Counting Rule

We have discussed how consistency is imposed on Model A through the imposing of the counting rule on the system. This is through an incorrect form of Say's Law being imposed on the system to eliminate a surplus equation. This incorrect Say's Law then restricts Model A to long-run states.

We need, of course, to ensure that price systems meet the counting rule. However, we need to apply this rule to Model A in a manner that does not result in the system being restricted to long-run states. This was accomplished in the following way.

We showed that Say's Law in being imposed on Model A ensures that the system meets the counting rule. However, the Law also ensures that Model A consistent with limitation in resources.

This brings inconsistency into the system; since consistency of the system with limitation in resources should be ensured by the behavior in the system.

This meant that if we could find a behavioral means to ensure consistency of Model A with limited resources, we would avoid having to impose Say's Law on the system to hence avoid the system's inconsistency.

Nonetheless, this alternative behavioral approach to ensuring consistency of Model A with limitation in resources would yet have to ensure that the number of independent equations and unknowns are equal as called for by the counting rule.

We established that this behavioral substitute for the counting rule is the new aspect to behavior described in Chapter 1.4 that we brought into Model B. This meant that this new aspect to behavior ensures consistency of Model B with limited resources.

Moreover, it also ensures consistency of Model B in ensuring equality between the number of independent equations and unknowns in the system.

Hence through this new aspect to behavior that we brought into Model B, we found a behavioral means of ensuring that the system meets the counting rule.

As a result, we do not have to *impose* consistency on Model B by imposing the counting rule on the system through Say's Law as has to be done in the case of Model A. This is because Model B meets the counting rule as a result of the system's behavior or economic rationale.

This difference between the systems accounts for Model A being restricted to long-run states by an incorrect form of Say's Law. On the other hand, Model B is not restricted by such an incorrect Say's Law to long-run states.

11.7 Indirectly Approaching Say's Law Through the New Aspect to behavior of Model B

Say's Law is a non-behavioral element that is imposed on Model A to eliminate a surplus equation to ensure consistency of the system. This as we have established accounts for the system being characterized by an incorrect or misused form of the Law that restricts the system to long-run states.

However, we cannot simply remove the Law from the system; since we would return to Model A in its initial state where it is characterized by a surplus equation over the number of unknowns.

We had to rid Model A of its incorrect form of the Law by finding a behavioral substitute for this incorrect Law. Let us review how this was accomplished. We showed that the Law not only rids Model A of a surplus equation.

We established that the Law also suppresses an aspect to the behavior of individuals and firms in the system. This is the aspect to behavior that should ensure consistency of Model A with limitation in resources.

We then resolved this inconsistency through Model B by bringing the new aspect to behavior described in Chapter 1.4 into this system. This meant that the Law in Model B is rid of the invalid role imputed to the Law in Model A of ensuring consistency of the latter system with limitation in resources.

This accounted for Model B being rid of Model A's incorrect form of the Law that restricts the latter system to long-run states. This was confirmed by Model B being characterized by a correct identity form of the Law that cannot possibly restrict the system to long-run states.

This is because as we established in Chapters 2.7 and 6.3, the Law in Model B is solely a descriptive device in this system. We may also put this analysis in the following way.

We remove in Model B the incorrect role that Say's Law plays in Model A of ensuring consistency of the latter system with limitation in resources; and we give this role to the behavior of Model B. This accounts for consistency of Model B being ensured by the behavior in the system rather than by Say's Law as in

Model A. This means that Model B reflects the general economic logic of price systems whereas this logic is suppressed in Model A.

11.8 Summary

There is a basic theme running through this book which is that our revised classical system, Model B, is based wholly on economic principles or economic behavior. This is in the sense that there is no interference with these principles or behavior in Model B stemming from non-behavioral elements such as Say's Law.

On the other hand, the behavior or economic rationale of the orthodox classical system, Model A, is restricted by the non-behavioral Say's Law which limits the generality of the system.

We proceeded by first discussing how we may look on the inconsistency of Model A as causing a gap in the system's behavioral content. This assisted us in bringing out how Say's Law is misused in Model A.

This is because the *non-behavioral Law* is brought into the picture to fill the gap in the system's *behavioral content*. We also reviewed aspects of the controversies that arose in response to Patinkin's claim that Model A is inconsistent in an economic sense.

Chapter 12

Summarizing The Book

This summary of the book draws on the preface but puts the remarks in the preface in a more general manner and in the context of the formal analyses that have now been set out. We shall also briefly review a number of basic findings of the book and also discuss aspects of the book that should be developed in more detail.

To review, we have uncovered in this book an inconsistency in economic theory. This is an inconsistency that characterizes orthodox theoretical price systems and which suppresses the general economic logic of the systems.

We focused in much of the book on this inconsistency as it characterizes the orthodox classical system which is a long-run system. However, we set out a revised classical system through which we resolved the inconsistency in the orthodox classical system.

Yet while much of our focus was on the classical system, this was with the broader aim of isolating the general economic logic that should underlie all price systems including macroeconomic systems such as the Keynesian system.

Consequently, this book dealt with the general logic that should underlie all price systems rather than with the specific forms of behavior of individual systems.

As discussed, we developed a revised classical system; and a substantial part of our analysis was concerned with contrasting this revised classical system with the orthodox classical system and the Keynesian is system.

However, in contrasting these systems, we contrasted only the general logic of the systems rather than contrasting the specific forms of behavior of the systems.

Let us describe the inconsistency that we uncovered in orthodox price systems, systems that we represented by the orthodox classical system, Model A.

Price systems are necessarily *subject* to limitation in resources. Hence the behavior in the systems should be behavior that ensures that the systems are *consistent* with limitation in resources.

We defined this as behavior that ensures that the quantities of commodities demanded and supplied in price systems, in being limited by the systems' given resources, each sum to the systems' limited or given resources in order to exhaust these resources.

Next, since consistency with limitation in resources applies across all price systems, we may look on consistency with limited resources as reflecting the general logic of the systems.

To review, we took the orthodox classical system, which we referred to as Model A, as representative of orthodox microeconomic price systems. As well, we set out a revised classical system which we referred to as Model B and which we took as representative of our new microeconomic systems.

Let us now consider the orthodox classical system Model A which we set out in detail in Chapter 3. We found that the behavior in this system does not ensure that the system is consistent with limitation in resources.

This is because an aspect to the behavior of individuals and firms which we described in Chapter 1.4 is missing from Model A. This is the aspect to behavior that should ensure that the system is consistent with limitation in resources. Next, all price systems must reflect consistency with limitation in resources.

Hence since the aspect to behavior referred to is missing from Model A, this resulted in the system being made consistent with limitation in resources in a non-behavioral manner. This is through Say's Law being imposed on Model A to eliminate a surplus equation to ensure that the system meets the counting rule. This brought inconsistency into Model A.

This is because consistency of a system with limitation in resources, or consistency of the system's general logic, should be ensured by the behavior in the system and hence by the system's demand and supply functions.

Model A, however, is made consistent with limitation in resources in a non-behavioral manner through Say's Law rather than by the behavior in the system. Model A does indeed reflect the *general logic* of price systems in reflecting consistency with limitation in resources.

However, Model A does not reflect the general *economic* logic of price systems; since consistency of the system with limitation in resources is not ensured by the behavior in the system. Instead, consistency with limitation in resources is ensured in a non-behavioral manner. This accounted for the inconsistency we have uncovered in the system.

Let us now consider our revised form of Model A which we referred to as Model B. We found that consistency with limitation in resources is ensured in Model B by the system's behavior or economic rationale. This meant that Model B, unlike Model A reflects the general *economic* logic of price systems.

Hence through Model B, our revised classical system, we resolved the inconsistency of Model A. This is because we brought the aspect to behavior that is missing from Model A into Model B. We may summarize the analysis of this book in the following way.

We established that the general logic of Model A, as reflected in consistency of the system with limitation in resources, is ensured in a non-behavioral manner rather than by the behavior in the system. This brought inconsistency into Model A since this system does not reflect the general *economic* logic that should underlie all price systems.

Whereas we established that the general logic of Model B, as also reflected in consistency of the system with limitation in resources, stems from the system's behavior or economic rationale. This meant that Model B, unlike Model A, reflects the general *economic* logic that should characterize all price systems.

This accounted for us resolving through Model B, the inconsistency of Model A; and through Model B, we came upon a more general approach to price systems compared to the orthodox approach that characterizes Model A.

This is due to Model B reflecting the new aspect to behavior described in Chapter 1.4 and hence the general economic logic that should characterize all price systems.

On the other hand, this new aspect to behavior and hence this general economic logic is missing from Model A which restricts the generality of the latter system compared to Model B.

This difference between the systems accounted for Model B being characterized by a more general approach to microeconomics compared to the orthodox approach to microeconomics of Model A. Let us illustrate this by contrasting the two systems.

In resolving the inconsistency of Model A through Model B, we rid the latter system of Model A's Say's Law. This is a form of the Law that restricts Model A to long-run states. Hence it is through Model B's more general economics that we rid this system of Model A's Say's Law.

Consequently, Model B has a more general character than Model A; since Model B is not restricted like Model A to long-run states by Say's Law. Let us now bring out some implications of this analysis for the Keynesian system.

Model B and the Keynesian system are both rid of Model A's Say's Law which restricts the latter system to long-run states. However, as discussed, we accomplish this through ridding Model B of the inconsistency we uncover in Model A.

This is by our approaching Model B through microeconomic analysis which accounts for the system being wholly microeconomic in character.

Keynes also rid his system of Model A's form of Say's Law that restricts the latter system to long-run states but this is accomplished through macroeconomic analysis. This is through Keynes allowing the aggregate demand and supply of commodities in his system to diverge.

This accounts for the microeconomics of the real part of the Keynesian system being suppressed this being the part of the system that deals with aggregate demand and supply variables. Hence we arrived at a similar conclusion through Model B and the Keynesian system.

This is that both of these systems are rid of Model A's Say's Law that restricts the latter system to long-run states. However, we accomplished this through microeconomic analysis whereas Keynes accomplished this through macroeconomic analysis.

This means that Keynes' macroeconomics is, as it were, a short-cut to ridding his system of Model A's form of Say's Law. This, however, is a short-cut that is forced on the Keynesian system. Let us discuss why this is the case.

Through Model B we resolved the inconsistency of Model A; and in so doing, we came upon a more general approach to microeconomics compared to the orthodox approach of Model A. This more general approach to microeconomics allowed us to rid Model B of Model A's Say's Law that restricts the latter system to long-run states.

Consequently, through Model B we avoided Keynes' macroeconomic short-cut to ridding his system of Model A's Say's Law. This short-cut accounts for the microeconomics of the real part of the Keynesian system being suppressed.

On the other hand, we rid Model B of Model A's Say's Law through microeconomic analysis. This accounts for Model B being wholly microeconomic in character. Hence we rid Model B of Model A's Say's Law while preserving Model B as a wholly microeconomic system.

Whereas Keynes rid his system of Model A's Say's Law in a manner that accounts for the microeconomics of the real part of the Keynesian system being suppressed. We can now bring out the overall consequences of the inconsistency of Model A for this system and the Keynesian system.

This inconsistency mars Model A by accounting for this system being restricted to long-run states by Say's Law. This inconsistency, however, was resolved through Model B. Hence this latter system is not restricted by the Law to long-run states. Let us next consider the Keynesian system.

Keynes as we discussed in Chapter 8 bypassed rather than resolve the inconsistency of Model A. This accounts for the Keynesian system being rid of Model A's Say's Law that restricts the latter system to long-run states. However, Keynes' approach results in the microeconomics of the real part of the Keynesian system being suppressed.

On the other hand, through Model B we resolved rather than bypass the inconsistency of Model A. This accounted for Model B being wholly microeconomic in character. We have now brought out the essential contribution of this book.

This is that in resolving through Model B the inconsistency we uncovered in Model A we arrived through Model B at a more general approach to microeconomics compared to the microeconomics of Model A.

This is on account of the new aspect behavior that we brought into Model B, an aspect to behavior that is missing from orthodox systems.

This accounted for us resolving through Model B, the problem of Model A being restricted to long-run states by Say's Law. Moreover, this is accomplished while ensuring that Model B is wholly microeconomic in character.

Keynes also resolved the problem of Model A being restricted to long-run states by Say's Law. Keynes, however, did not accomplish this by resolving the inconsistency of Model A as is done in this book. Instead, Keynes through his macroeconomic approach bypassed this inconsistency in his system.

This approach allowed Keynes to rid his system of the problem of Model A being restricted to long-run states by Say's Law. However, this is accomplished in a manner that accounts for the microeconomics of the real part of the Keynesian system being suppressed. There is a further key part of our analysis that we shall now review.

We arrived at a more general approach to price systems through Model B by resolving through the latter system, the inconsistency we uncover in Model A. This, to review, is an inconsistency concerning how consistency with limitation in resources is ensured in this system. Next, consistency of price systems with limitation in resources is ensured through the systems' budget constraints.

This meant that our resolving through Model B the inconsistency of Model A concerning how consistency with limitation in resources of the latter system is ensured was reflected in our dealing with the systems' budget constraints in the following way.

This is through our dealing with Model B's budget constraint in a more general manner compared to how Model A's budget constraint is dealt with. Let us review this analysis.

We found that the new aspect to behavior that we brought into Model B broadens the meaning of the overall output or income variable of this system to also reflect the system's limited flow of resources.

Next, since budget constraints arise as a result of limitation in resources, Model B's overall output or income variable provides the basis for the system's budget constraint. Now this overall output or income variable is determined by behavioral market processes in Model B.

Consequently, Model B's budget constraint is determined by the system's behavioral market processes. Hence this budget constraint in being determined within the system cannot possibly restrict Model B to long-run states. Let us now consider Model A.

Model A lacks the new aspect to behavior that we bring into Model B that broadens the meaning of the overall output or income variable of the latter system to also reflect the system's limited flow of resources. Yet Model A's overall output or income also provides the basis for a budget constraint in the system.

However, Model A's overall output or income is not determined by behavioral market processes as in Model B but by non-behavioral market processes that stem from Say's Law. This meant that Model A's budget constraint is not determined within the system by behavioral market processes as in Model B.

This accounted for Model A being characterized by an external budget constraint that restricts the system to long-run states. This analysis explained why Model A is restricted in generality compared to Model B; since as discussed, the latter system's internal budget constraint cannot possibly restrict this system to long-run states.

This analysis also explained why Model A is characterized by an incorrect form of Say's Law that is not a true identity that restricts this system to long-run states. This is because as discussed in Chapter 9.4, this incorrect Say's Law enters Model A on account of the system's external budget constraint.

Moreover, this analysis also explained why Model B is characterized by a correct form of Say's Law that is a true identity that cannot possibly restrict this system to long-run states. This is because as also discussed in Chapter 9.4 this correct Say's Law enters Model A on account of the system's internal budget constraint.

This book has focused on bringing out the general economic logic that should underlie all price systems. This was by our focusing on the long-run Model B but we also dealt with the Keynesian system which is a short-run system.

However, we dealt with the Keynesian system only to the extent that it deals with issues relevant to the general logic that should underlie all price systems. Let us now bring together strands of the preceding analyses to bring out the overall rationale of the book.

Model A is initially inconsistent in that it does not initially meet the counting rule since there is a surplus equation over the number of unknowns. Say's Law is then imposed on the system to eliminate a surplus equation to ensure consistency of the system.

This however, as we discussed earlier results in an incorrect form of the Law being imposed on the system that restricts it to long-run states. This is because Model A is made consistent by the non-behavioral Say's Law rather than by the behavior in the system.

To review, Model A is restricted in generality because consistency of the system with limitation in resources is ensured by the non-behavioral Say's Law. On the other hand, consistency of Model B with limitation in resources is ensured by the behavior in the system. This accounts for Model B having a more general character than Model A.

This is reflected in various ways that we have discussed, for example, in Model B being rid of Model A's incorrect Say's Law that restricts the latter system to long-run states.the system that causes the system to be initially inconsistent. This then causes economists to impose Say's Law on the system.

Hence to rid the system of its incorrect Say's Law we need to look into the system's behavioral content. That is, into the system's demand and supply functions. It is in so doing that we came upon the economic inconsistency in Model A.

Next, as we shall now discuss, in resolving Model A's inconsistency through Model B, we rid the latter system of the Say's Law of Model A that restricts the latter system to long-run state.

Say's Law not only ensures consistency of Model A by eliminating a surplus equation from the system. We established that the Law also simultaneously ensures consistency of the system with limitation in resources.

This brought an economic inconsistency into Model A since consistency of the system with limitation in resources should be ensured by the behavior in the system. However, we resolved this inconsistency of Model A through Model B by bringing the new aspect to behavior described in Chapter 1.4 into the latter system.

This accounts for Model B automatically meeting the counting rule. Hence we did not need the Law to ensure consistency of Model B. Consequently, we rid the latter system of Model A's incorrect Say's Law that restricts this system to long-run states.

This was replaced in Model B with a correct identity form of the Law that cannot possible restrict the latter system to long-run states. This means that Model A is restricted in generality compared to Model A.

Most generally, this is because consistency of Model A is incorrectly ensured in being ensured by the non-behavioral Say's Law. On the other hand, consistency of Model B is correctly ensured in being ensured by the behavior in the system. There is a further stage to our analysis.

As we discussed, through bringing the new aspect to behavior described in Chapter 1.4 into Model B we brought a correct form of the Law into this system. Let establish more precisely how this was accomplished.

Model B's new aspect to behavior brings a correct identity form of the Law into Model B. This is by bringing an internal budget constraint into the system.

This internal budget constraint is a true identity form of the Law hence it cannot restrict Model B to long-run states. In contrast, the new aspect to behavior of Model B is absent from Model A.

This accounts for this latter system being characterized by an external budget constraint. This is not a true identity form of the Law; and it accounts for Model A being restricted to long-run states. In sum, much of the book turns on how consistency of Model A and Model B is ensured.

To review, Say's Law is imposed on Model A to eliminate a surplus equation to ensure that the system meets the counting rule. This very approach, however, brings an economic inconsistency into the system; since it accounts for consistency with limitation in resources being ensured in Model A in a non-behavioral manner rather than by the behavior in the system.

On the other hand, the new aspect to behavior of Model B ensures that the system meets the counting rule. This approach rids Model B of the economic inconsistency of Model A; since it accounts for consistency with limitation in resources being ensured in Model B by the behavior in the system.

Finally, we may confirm that Model B is rid of the inconsistency of Model A in the following way. This is through Model A being characterized by an external budget constraint form of Say's Law which is not a true identity; and this incorrect form of the Law restricts the system to long-run states.

On the other hand, Model B is characterized by an internal budget constraint form of Say's Law which is a true identity; and this correct form of the Law cannot possibly restrict this system to long-run states. Let us now list some of the basic findings of the book.

We set out in Chapter 1.4 the new aspect to behavior that we brought into Model B through which we resolved the inconsistency we uncovered in Model A. Next, we discussed in Chapter 4.7 how Keynes and Patinkin dealt only with symptoms or consequences of the inconsistency of Model A rather than with this inconsistency itself as is done in this book.

In Chapter 8.6 we focused on how the variable W is dealt with in Model A, Model B and the Keynesian system. This allowed us to bring out how Keynes bypassed the inconsistency in Model A. Then in Chapter 9.5 we contrasted how Model B is rid of Model A's incorrect form of Say's Law with how Keynes rid his system of this form of the Law.

We also brought out in Chapter 9.6 a basic issue with Keynes' approach to the classical system and Say's Law. To review, the orthodox classical system, Model A, is restricted to long-run states by a form of the Law which we established is an incorrect or misused form of the Law.

Keynes then wholly removed Model A's Say's Law from his system. This meant that the Keynesian system is not restricted by the Law to long-run states hence it can move to alternative states as behavior changes, a reflection of the system's macroeconomic character.

However, while Model A's incorrect Say's Law does indeed restrict the system to long-run states the solution to this is not simply to rid this system of this incorrect form of the Law. We need to ask the question of why, in the first place, an incorrect form of the Law entered Model A?

193

Through pursuing this question, we uncovered that an incorrect form of Say's Law entered Model A because of the inconsistency we uncovered in the system. This inconsistency arose because Model A lacks the new aspect to behavior described in Chapter 1.4.

However, we brought this new aspect behavior into Model B. Hence through the latter system we resolved the inconsistency of Model A. This accounted for Model B being rid of Model A's incorrect Say's Law in a manner that ensured that Model B is wholly microeconomic in character.

On the other hand, Keynes rid his system of Model A's Say's Law in a manner that resulted in the microeconomics of the real part of the Keynesian system being suppressed. There were other basic findings of the book.

Patinkin held that Model A is characterized by an indeterminate price level and invalid real-monetary dichotomy. However, these problems with Model A that were brought out by Patinkin were resolved in Chapters 10.3 and 10.4 through a monetary form of Model B.

This as through our establishing that only relative commodity demands and relative commodity supplies can be determined independently of the monetary sector in the classical system.

This allowed us to contrast Model A and Model B in the following way: the real sector of Model B determines only $(n-1)$ *relative* commodity demands (supplies).

On the other hand, the real sector of Model A determines *absolute* commodity demands (supplies) for all n commodities. Consequently, Walras Law can operate in Model B when the system is out of equilibrium but not in Model A.

We dealt with Model B as a market system hence we did not develop it in detail from the maximizing behavior of the individual and the firm underlying the system.

However, while we did not develop Model B from this maximizing behavior, we may look on this book as dealing, through Model B, with how a consistent transition from this maximizing behavior to the theory of market price determination may be made.

This transition would require using the quantities of commodities demanded and supplied by each individual and firm that are derived from their maximizing behavior, to form demand and supply functions that apply to each

194

individual and firm. We may then impose on these functions, the new aspect to behavior described in Chapter 1.4.

This would give these functions a behavioral relative character. These functions of the individual and the firm may then be aggregated to form the market demand and supply functions of Model B, our revised classical system.

We would, of course, now have to take the distribution of income and other resources among individuals and firms explicitly into account which has not been done in this book.

Next we brought out in Chapter 9.11 how Keynes' analysis implies that there is an internal budget constraint in his macroeconomic system. However, we did not go fully into the implications of this for the Keynesian system. This, however, should be done in more detailed forms of our analysis.

These more detailed analyses would need to formally set out this Keynesian internal budget constraint and cover various implications of this budget constraint for the Keynesian system, implications that we have not addressed in this book.

This book has focused on bringing out the general economic logic that should underlie all price systems; and we accomplished this through our revised classical system, Model B, which is a long-run system. However, short-run forms of this system should be developed but this was beyond the scope of the present book.

Clearly, however, Model B provides the basis to form short-run systems of considerable generality. This is because since Model B is not restricted by Say's Law to long-run states, the system in principle can move into short-run states were behavior to change to short-run behavior.

We may form short-run versions of Model B by using the approach of the latter system to form short-run systems. These short-run systems unlike short-run or macroeconomic systems such as the Keynesian system will like Model B be wholly microeconomic in character.

Moreover, short-run forms of Model B will reflect like the latter system, the general economic logic that should characterize all price systems. This general economic logic stems from the new aspect to behavior described in Chapter 1.4.

This new aspect to behavior is of such generality that it not only allowed us to resolve the inconsistency we uncovered in the orthodox classical system. This new aspect to behavior applies across all price systems and, in principle, it can bring an underlying unity to price systems irrespective of the differing forms of behavior of individual systems. Q.E.D.

Index